Tilly

The ugliest cat in the shelter

How I rescued her and she rescued me

Celia Haddon

hamlyn

This book is dedicated to Roger Coffin,

a wonderful teacher, who did what even Tilly could not do.

He taught me statistics.

Contents

Chapter 1

I find the ugliest cat

'This must be the ugliest cat in Oxfordshire,' said my husband, Ronnie, as he looked at the small photo on my camera.

'She's not that ugly,' I protested.

'She's the colour of sewage and what about those ears! She looks as if she's really unfriendly.'

'She's not the colour of sewage. Mud, maybe, but not sewage,' I argued.

It was summer 2010 and Ronnie was in a hospital bed, waiting for an operation that would graft skin on to a severe leg wound. He had fallen down the stairs and cut his leg on a picture frame that fell with him. It was a deep wound, and as he was 84 years old, the hospital doctors were not anxious to operate on him. As a former Royal Marine commando, he was gung-ho keen that they should.

I visited him every afternoon. The hospital ward was full of men aged 50 and upwards. Opposite him was Adam, a retired gardener in his eighties, confused and unable to feed himself except with his fingers. Next door was a very ill man who just lay quietly in bed. Across at an angle was a cheerful guy, John, who was waiting for an operation and in trouble with the nurses for sneaking out to the pub for a drink the day before.

For a couple of days I had kept quiet about the new cat in the spare bedroom, because Ronnie had been so ill and at times quite out of his mind. He spent one night shouting that the hospital nurses were trying to kill him and that the ward had been infiltrated by a terrorist cell. His earlier years as a terrorism expert and war correspondent had resurfaced in his mind, as an infection made the wrong brain cells fire up. All night he was the patient from hell.

The following day was only a little better. He had some horrible hallucinations about former US President George Bush, of all people. Then he decided he was back in the *Daily Telegraph* newsroom as a war reporter, and would call over the nurses to say, 'You are not covering this story properly. Why aren't you sending me?' John, across the ward, was forgiving about the shouting, and took a certain satisfaction at hearing the nurses who had rebuked him for his trip to the pub being rebuked in their turn for poor journalism! However, I thought I had better wait until Ronnie was a bit more able to cope before telling him about Tottie.

I too was very stressed. Ronnie is the love of my life and we had been together for more than 40 years. I hated seeing him on the hospital ward, particularly a geriatric ward. In my eyes, he is still the dashing war correspondent I first met, not an old man.

I don't trust hospitals – doctors, nurses or the food. Every day I would bring in something for him to eat, and try to entertain him a little. I would also attempt to read his notes so I could wise up on his medication. I would pester the nurses for information, double checking everything they told me via Google when I got home.

My stress hormones were sky high and I was afloat with adrenaline. Naturally, I couldn't sleep at night as my mind was obsessively worrying about Ronnie. After any week of hospital visiting – and I have now done more than I like to remember – I am a highly energized, all-singing, all-dancing wreck of a wife.

The day I decided to break the news about Tottie, Ronnie was recovering a bit. He was able to think straight – a good sign. I had brought in my camera to show him my new foster cat, Tottie.

It seems mad that I had even thought of taking on a foster cat while his health crisis was going on. It was not a sensible decision in any way. My stress levels were so intense that a new and difficult cat was only going to make things worse.

Some people turn to alcohol to deal with stress. Others eat their way through huge mounds of carbohydrates. Still others rely on prescription drugs or even on street drugs. When stressed, I turn either to scientific papers about cats (I am a reference nerd) or to cats themselves. I had no particular writing project or science assignment on hand, so it had to be cats this time. A challenging cat project was just what I needed. Or so I told myself. As cat lovers know, there's always an excuse for a new cat!

Ronnie, however, was not keen on any new cat. I had converted him to cats with difficulty over the years we had been together, and he was still not a reliable disciple, liable to backslide on the question of pets in the home. Thirty years earlier, a black-and-white mother cat had turned up in our garden and given birth to a single kitten there. We later called her Ada because she looked like a housemaid in a smart black-and-white uniform.

I had suckered Ronnie into adopting, or rather letting me adopt, Ada, our first cat. He was cat neutral because he had grown up in a household entirely without pets – no cats, no dogs, not even a rabbit. I saw this as a huge deprivation for any child but he disagreed. 'It never entered my head to want to own a cat or a dog,' he told me. 'There was a dog I used to take for walks as a child, but I only did it for pocket money. I didn't want one of my own.'

'Besides,' he added, 'I enjoy a cat-free ambience.' His later adult life had left little space for cats, anyway. A cat-free (his phrase, not mine) childhood was followed by equally cat-free years spent first as a Royal Marine commando in World War Two, then as an undergraduate at Oxford University, and finally as a foreign correspondent and war reporter for the *Daily Telegraph*. The front line was no place for people with cats.

So he was never going to be enthusiastic about the acquisition of Tottie. For the first time in ages, he had been enjoying several weeks of 'cat-free ambience' again. My phrase for it was 'cat deprivation'. Our last cat, William, had suffered from cancer of the tongue and had been put to sleep the previous autumn. We had not taken on a permanent cat since his death. I had been too busy, finishing a science degree in animal behaviour, and collecting, reading and referencing scientific papers like a mad thing. My research obsession had temporarily taken the place of cat obsession.

Then just a few days after my final exams, Ronnie took the tumble that landed him in hospital. He had, although I found it difficult to believe, positively enjoyed the preceding weeks without a cat. He was not keen on becoming a cat owner again, least of all with this particular ugly cat.

I don't think Ronnie had fully recovered from the loss of William seven months earlier. He had loved William. We had adopted him from a household in Somerset, which contained 54 cats. While the house was clean and free from faeces, every flat surface had one or more cats on it. They sat and lounged or slept on tables, shelves, chairs, armchairs and kitchen surfaces, mostly with just a few inches of space between them. Almost as many cats remained on the floor, hiding under beds, under sofas, behind the TV, and squeezed under chests of drawers. These were the unhappiest of cats, stressed out of their minds by the presence of so many others. For them, it was like being thrown into the middle of a crowd of hostile strangers – the smells, the sights and the noises of so many other cats terrified them.

Ronnie chose William from a basket of kittens. 'I liked the way he kept climbing out on to the rim of the basket,' he explained. 'He would fall off back into the basket and just start climbing up again. He was really persistent.'

At one point in William's fourteen years of life, Ronnie started dreaming about him. One dream was particularly vivid. 'William was wearing a Marine beret,' reported Ronnie. 'And I heard somebody nearby, possibly me, saying, "He's a very gallant officer."' When he told me this, I realized that Ronnie was in thrall to William. His unconscious mind had made William a member of his regiment. That green beret was the sign of total approval!

William had grown into a glamorous tabby-and-white cat. His hair was longish, just long enough to be beautiful and not so long that he had to be brushed twice a day. He had glorious whiskers, a gorgeous fluffy tail, huge soft paws with fur between the pads, and a very gentle disposition. He was so handsome that I even won a photographic competition with his portrait. For sheer elegance and beauty, William was a hard feline act to follow.

Tottie didn't come anywhere close in looks. She *was* ugly. The photograph on my camera showed a cat cowering in the cat pen, shrunk into the furthest part of the sleeping compartment. Her ears were back flat on her skull and her eyes were huge with fear. Her coat was more stringy than fluffy, brown with yellow patches, and no white anywhere. Only the tufts of dark hair coming out of her ears were attractive. Otherwise she did not make a pretty photograph, even though I had tried to show her looking better than she actually was. The flash from the camera had turned her eyes golden, with bright gold pupils, but in reality her eyes were a pale frog-coloured green.

'You wait till I'm helpless in hospital to spring this ugly cat on me,' grumbled Ronnie.

'She's only a foster cat,' I said to him, knowing it was pointless to argue about her looks. 'She's coming to our home for rehabilitation. I'm going to help her get used to domestic life. Then she'll find a new home. I'm not going to adopt her. I'm just going to pass her on.'

'It's not fair,' he replied. 'If you really have to bring a feline lodger into the house, why can't we have a nice little kitten? Cardinal Richelieu had the right idea. He had pretty little kittens in his palaces, not adult cats. If we must have another cat, I want another kitten like William.'

He was right about one thing. I *had* waited until he was in hospital before taking Tottie home. I knew if he'd had any say in it, Tottie would never have entered our house at all. She was not just ugly; she was also one of the most frightened cats I had ever come across. The photograph I showed Ronnie was the best one of scores I had taken. She looked awful in them all. Like most people, Ronnie judges a cat on its looks. Hers were dire. He also took against her name. 'It sounds like the name of an Edwardian music-hall singer,' was his tetchy comment. 'And a bad one at that!' Then he added, 'She looks like George Bush. She's got his eyes and face!' Coming after his George Bush hallucinations, this was not a compliment. In other circumstances, Ronnie might admire George Bush but not on this particular occasion.

I took a second look at my photograph on the camera. Were the eyes and face similar? Obviously her whiskered cheeks were nothing like Bush's clean-shaven cheeks. How would the former president have looked if he'd had black whiskers and tortoiseshell fur on his face? It was difficult to make the imaginative jump.

'I don't think she looks at all like George Bush,' I said firmly. 'You're inventing a likeness.'

The photo had not helped reconcile him to our new house guest. A good photo sells a difficult cat and she was a difficult cat to sell as a family pet. Like a bed blocker in a hospital, Tottie had been taking up space for too long in the care of our Cats Protection branch. I had done my best to make her look good for the website picture, visiting her on three separate occasions to try to take a photo that would made her look mildly attractive, but to no avail.

I am a member of a small branch of this excellent charity. We home about 170 cats and kittens each year. The branch struggles to survive. Hard-working volunteers arrange jumble sales, man stalls at village fetes, run raffles and organize tombolas to raise money. Photos on the website are what encourages most people to adopt one of our cats. Rescuing unwanted cats, such as Tottie, is an expensive business and the longer they stay with us the more they cost us. Each cat has to be vet checked, treated for fleas and mites, and neutered before being homed. Stray cats that are picked up from the street, or caught roaming country areas, often need so much medical treatment that the bill can run to four figures. Sometimes these unwanted cats, already ill, are deliberately dumped to take their chance, because owners cannot or will not get them veterinary treatment.

When I first saw her, Tottie was living in a pen with a long-haired, glamorous tortoiseshell-and-white cat named Lottie. The pens were in the back garden of a volunteer, Ann. Cats Protection has large adoption centres round Britain but small branches, such as ours, have fosterers who take cats into their own homes or have one or two cat pens in their back garden.

The two cats had come from the same home originally, and were meant to be friends, but as Tottie spent most of her time trying to hide in her bed, it did not look as if their friendship was very cordial. Humans often overestimate the degree of friendship between cats. The best you could say about this pair was that they didn't fight.

Lottie was friendly to humans and enjoyed it when Ann stroked and brushed her. Ann lives in a Cotswold village in an ideal spot for cats, away from traffic. As you turn into her driveway, you usually see a cat or two wandering around. These are her own pets, mostly cats unable to find a home. She has several but she hasn't gone too far. Her house backs on to green fields so there is plenty of territory for them. The garden is long and large, too. Her house is always spotlessly clean despite the felines – cleaner and tidier than mine. Ann is devoted to cats but sensible about them. She does the accounts for our branch and is one of the most hard-working and kindest people I know.

Some cat fosterers end up with too many cats because they can't bear to see their fostered felines go to another home. They fall in love with them and cannot part from them. Ann stays the right side of sanity on this issue – even if one of her current cats, Moses, is a black-and-white terror, completely feral, who won't give humans the time of day.

When I turned up with my camera to take pictures for the website, Lottie looked really wonderful. She had a white face with golden eyes, long shining fur, a little pink nose and long white whiskers, and she came towards me with interest. She was clearly a 'people' cat.

Tottie simply shrank away from me as far as possible, looking fearful. Taking a photo was a hopeless task on the first occasion. The two cats were difficult even to get into the same frame, because they were sitting so far apart, clearly not wishing to be close to each other. The photo showed glamorous Lottie in the forefront with Tottie cowering in her bed in the furthest part of the pen.

'These aren't very good photos,' I said to Ann. 'I'll come back another day and try again when I have more time.'

I decided that, on my next visit, I would sit in the pen long enough for both cats to get used to me. When I arrived, Ann was out. Her husband let me into the cat pen and went back to mowing the lawn.

The photo session did not go well. Lottie was immediately interested by the camera and kept walking too close to it. Tottie, obviously upset by the lawn-mower noise, appeared to be even more terrified than before. Her hair practically stood out in spikes, like a cartoon cat, and her ears were flatter back on her head, if that was possible.

If you saw these photographs – and I have kept just one – you would think, 'What a beautiful cat!' as your eye fell on Lottie. Then you would spy Tottie, cowering in the background. The photographs showed a muddy looking scaredy cat; not the sort of cat anybody would want.

The two were to be homed together, and nobody had volunteered to take both of them. Even Lottie's good looks could not sell poor Tottie's bad ones. The pair had been in the pen for a year and a half. Adopters wouldn't take Lottie, because the price was taking Tottie as well.

Kittens, not adult cats, are what most adopters want. Nothing wrong in that and every summer Cats Protection finds homes for scores of kittens. They are the stars of any cat rescue. Usually, when we have a mother and kittens, the kittens are adopted before the mother. Kittens rock!

People call us in when they come across a stray who has given birth under a bush, or in their garden shed, or behind the dustbins. We take in mum and her kittens and find homes for all of them. These babies, were we not to rescue them, would grow up to be wild animals, not domesticated felines. We call such cats feral. Ferals are difficult to tame and rarely make good family pets.

Neither Tottie nor Lottie had the star quality of kittens, although, luckily for them, they were still relatively young. Elderly cats have the least chance of adoption. Only a few specially loving humans will give them a warm fireside for the rest of their lives. Despite making very good indoor-only cats, the old ones may need to wait for months and months for a home. In theory, because she was young, Tottie should have been adopted much quicker.

It can only have been the fault of her muddy colour and terrified body language that nobody had wanted her. After age, colour matters to would-be adopters. Most people choose cats because of their looks, particularly their colour. Prejudice among adopters puts any dark animals looking for a home at a severe disadvantage. Animal shelters all know that BBUs and SBUs – Big Black Uglies in the case of dogs and Small Black Uglies in the case of cats – are difficult to home.

Pale-coloured cats are chosen first. Smokey blue or Siamese colours are popular. White, ginger or ginger-and-white cats also find homes fast. Then come the tabby and whites and the all-over tabbies. Tabby cats, particularly light rather than dark ones, seem popular with almost everybody. Perhaps it's the stripes and blotches.

Next in popularity come black-and-white cats. Much depends on their markings. A nice white shirt front with matching white paws makes some cats look as smart as Fred Astaire in his dancing coat tails. These cats have style. Other black-and-white cats have markings that make people laugh and adopt them. There is a whole website devoted to cats that look like Hitler, with black markings like small moustaches (www.catsthatlooklikehitler.com). Hitler cats, sometimes known as 'kitlers', will usually find a home among people who enjoy the joke.

Least popular are black or brown cats. Tabbies are twice as likely to be adopted. Black cats are thought to be unlucky in the United States and are very unpopular there. I met a veterinary nurse who had worked at an American cat shelter in the 1990s, and she told me that the unpopularity of black cats was particularly upsetting at Halloween. Apparently, there's a belief in America that black cats are burned alive at Halloween by practitioners of black magic. Well-meaning members of the public would hand in black cats to her animal shelter, thinking to save them from an awful death. Instead, these 'rescued' cats were immediately put to sleep. Here in the UK, where well-run charities, such as Cats Protection, do not put down healthy cats, black cats are not killed. They just spend months confined in a small cat pen, waiting for somebody who is willing to take them home.

So where do tortoiseshell cats, such as Lottie and Tottie, rank in popularity? If they have some white on them, they are as popular as the tabbies and tabby and whites. Tortoiseshell-and-white cats, such as Lottie, are normally female, just as ginger cats are normally male, and are adopted fast if they have nice markings. Lottie was very glamorous. If she hadn't been offered as a package with Tottie, she would have found a new home quickly.

Brown tortoiseshells without any white, like Tottie, are unpopular. These dark tortoiseshells look brown at a distance, and brown cats, according to one American survey, are even slower to be adopted than black ones.

So Tottie was always going to be bottom of the list for adoption. Adopters who like the look of a cat will talk of 'falling in love' with the cat of their dreams. Like falling in love with humans, adopting a cat is often not so much a rational decision as an emotional one. Ugly brown cats just don't hit that love spot for most would-be adopters.

The fact that Tottie was female didn't help, either. Male cats are adopted quicker than females. Neither was her long hair helpful. While people may like long-haired pedigree cats, they are less likely to take on a long-haired ordinary domestic moggy. All that daily brushing puts them off.

So Tottie's prospects were poor. Even the black cats handed in to our Cats Protection branch were finding homes before Lottie and Tottie. It wasn't just that Tottie was the least desirable colour. Had she behaved nicely, coming up to the front of the pen purring, somebody would have taken both cats on the strength of Lottie's appeal, but one look at Tottie skulking in her cat bed had persuaded would-be adopters to give both cats a miss. She looked aggressive and suspicious. In fact, she was merely terrified.

Finally, in desperation, Cats Protection decided to let the two cats be adopted separately. At least this way one of the cats would find a home. Lottie was adopted almost immediately. Tottie was left on the shelf. Neither Ann nor I were surprised. But it was good to know that Lottie had finally found a home of her own, and even better when her new owner called to say what a wonderful cat she was. For Lottie, this was a happy ending to her early difficulties and, as we always hope, the beginning of a lifetime spent in a home of safety and love.

Now Tottie was all on her own. Alas, it made little difference to her behaviour. She still quailed in her bed if an unknown human came near. We began to wonder if she was feral. Cats Protection does not put ferals to sleep. Normally, our branch finds homes for these undomesticated cats as mousers. Farmers and stable owners find that a couple of healthy cats will keep down rats and mice.

Our feral cats are neutered, treated for worms and fleas, and sent out to lead a hunter's life somewhere where there is proper shelter. They must be fed properly, too, since fed cats catch more mice. Hunger simply weakens them and makes them less efficient hunters. For feral cats, terrified of humans, life on a farm or in a stable is the best life of all. Hunting mice is what Nature designed them to do.

This was the life that might have been Tottie's, but for one problem – her long fluffy coat. Her fur was of the kind found in pedigree Birman cats. The strong tough hairs that protect the surface of the feline coat, the so-called guard hairs, were missing. Instead, she had a coat made up entirely of undercoat, the soft fluffy hairs that don't keep out the weather. Moreover, this kind of fluffy coat becomes knotted and matted very easily and needs regular grooming.

Feral stable cats do not let anybody near enough to groom them. If we just let Tottie live in outbuildings or a stable, she would end up matted all over. Mats on a cat are a health issue. As the fur knots and tangles, it tightens and pulls. Under the mats, the skin becomes sore and may even split open and bleed.

So Tottie couldn't be adopted as a farm cat, yet nobody wanted her as a pet. She behaved as if she wasn't keen on being a pet, either. Her future was not bright. If she had been in some of the American shelters, she would probably have been euthanized early on. Some US shelters put more than half their cats to sleep because they can find homes for only a few of them. But thanks to Cats Protection's no-kill policy, Tottie was still alive 18 months after being handed in to us; alive, but with a poor quality of life. While some cats manage well in a cat pen, Tottie was clearly very stressed by it, and it looked as if she was going to be stuck there for life. Who on earth would want an ugly cat who shrank away from humans?

'It occurred to me that you might be able to help,' said Ann hesitantly, when we were discussing Tottie's plight. I had come to make a third attempt to take an attractive, or perhaps just a less unattractive, photo of the small cat.

Ann had taken away the green plastic cat bed and left the fleece in the corner of the bed area, so that Tottie was now more visible. You could see more of her cringing back, lowered head and flat ears. She was the classic frightened cat, trying to make herself look as small as she possibly could. Her body was pressed as low to the ground as she could manage, her paws were tucked away underneath her, her tail was tightly wound around her body and those ears were laid back. Her eyes were dilated with terror. Photographically speaking, it was hopeless. She still looked awful.

'Perhaps,' said Ann tentatively, 'you could foster her in your home. She might be able to get used to people better there. Then perhaps she would have a better chance of adoption.'

'She'd have a better chance of adoption with a better name,' I said. 'I can't bear the name Tottie. Can I call her Tilly instead? It might help.' So after I had taken her home, and Ronnie had made it clear that he too hated the name, Tottie became Tilly. Renaming was the first step towards what we hoped might be a better future for her.

Next was the problem of her terrified behaviour. The idea of trying to change that was tempting to me. I had just finished studying for a science degree in applied animal behaviour and was anxious to practise my newly learned skills while I waited to see if I had got my degree.

Tottie, now Tilly, would be an interesting case. Her future, unless she changed, was bleak. Some cat rescue organizations would have been tempted to put her down. Even if I failed to change her behaviour completely, she would at least learn what it was like to live in a home with people. Perhaps she would even manage to get used to humans in her territory.

It seemed unlikely she would ever learn to love us. That was too much to hope. And I wouldn't learn to love such an unlovable cat, either. Instead, as a newly qualified cat behaviourist, I could work on her behaviour in a detached, scientific way. She would be a challenge. Neither of us had much to gain but the transaction was an interesting one to me and might do her some good.

'Why not?' I said to Ann, which is how I came to take on the ugliest and most frightened cat in our branch of Cats Protection.

Chapter 2

How cats chose me

Why Tilly? I suppose that question contains three different ones. The first is just this – why do any of us humans keep pets at all? The second is why do I keep cats rather than horses, dogs, rabbits or even budgies. And finally, why on earth did I give a home to Tilly, the ugliest cat in the shelter, the cat nobody else wanted?

First, I am a pet-keeping animal, as are most humans. If you pause to think about it, it is weird that we adopt a different species into our families. Most pets, dogs and cats included, are not useful to us. They cost time and energy to rear and look after, and in Western society, they are expensive consumers of pet food and veterinary treatment.

Everywhere in the world there are humans who will adopt animals – not just dogs and cats, but monkeys, hippos, giraffes, lambs, squirrels, llamas, capybaras, mice and sparrows. Baby animals, in particular, seem to appeal to something instinctive in human beings. Just the look of a baby animal's face, especially if it is round with large eyes, a small nose and a pink mouth, makes us want to take care of the tiny creature. We are programmed to respond to baby faces. This is why adults coo over a pram. Nature provides babies with a face that appeals to adults because helpless human babies need mothering to survive.

Puppies and kittens both have somewhat similar baby-shaped faces when they are very young – rounded, large-eyed, small-nosed. We are designed to love baby faces and thus to love the animals that share this look. This partly explains why I love pets. I am instinctively drawn to them. It is in my human nature.

Then there is my nurture. I grew up on a farm surrounded with pets. During my childhood, my family kept dogs, rabbits, guinea pigs, white mice, canaries, a pet raven, pigeons, Java sparrows, tortoises, ponies, horses and donkeys. I also spent time with the young of the farmyard animals – piglets, lambs, calves and chicks – and at one time I regularly fed a wild rat who lived above one of the pig sties.

Samuel Whiskers, as I called him after a Beatrix Potter character, would emerge from his hole and run along a ledge at the back of the sty. He would grab the food I put there for him before running very fast back into his hole. As the weeks passed he grew sleek, and he would come out to take the food with growing confidence. I knew that nobody else loved rats but I could not help boasting about him.

'I have a new pet,' I announced at the family lunch table. Two days later Samuel Whiskers failed to show up. I should have kept him secret from the hostile adult world.

In my childhood home, of course, there were cats. All farmyards had cats in those days. You would walk into the farmyard and four or five cats would dash away into the barns. These were the semi-feral farm cats, living more or less wild lives but helped out with a saucer of milk or some food scraps left for them at the back door of the dairy. Inside the house, a kitchen cat usually held sway, twice as large and twice as fat as the farm cats, and very tame. This lucky animal would have been adopted as a kitten by the farmer's wife.

Our farm was one of three in a Berkshire village in the flat and fertile Thames valley. Its fields had been ploughed since Saxon times and, in the early 1950s, before the advent of artificial fertilizer, the farm still followed more or less the old three-year system. Corn was grown in a field for two years, and the straw used to bed down cattle (and my father's horses) in the winter. In the third year, the field was put down to lucerne or turnips, which were fed to cattle in their winter quarters.

In addition to growing wheat and oats (for the horses), we had a herd of milking cows, some pigs, and chickens that wandered all over the farmyard. Cattle yards had been constructed at the back of the older farm buildings. The farm's central yard, now given over to barn conversions, had a storage barn with old-fashioned cattle stalls on the right, and in the centre, a large barn, now with a modern grain dryer. On the left was the farm garden, at the end of which was the original 17th-century house. Behind the later Georgian rooms facing the garden were a flag-stoned dairy for making butter and cheese, a big kitchen and an equally large pantry. Past the dairy, a tack room and six loose boxes for my father's hunters stood near the pig sties.

The house and outbuildings were the territory of a dynasty of white cats. The founder and matriarch was my elder sister's cat Simpkin, who spent most of her leisure time sitting very close to the round hot plate of the coke-powered Aga stove in the red-flagged farm kitchen. Before central heating, the kitchen was the warmest room in the house. Simpkin had been spayed. In the 1950s we were ahead of our time in having not just our male cats castrated but also having the females spayed.

Looking back, I am impressed by this. Neutering females was a new idea, although male cats had been neutered for years. The pioneer in postwar Britain was Miss Nerea de Clifford, a big shot in the world of cats and author of *What British Cats Think About Television*. Her conclusion was that 'most cats show an interest of some kind though it is often one of hostility.' In common with other formidable women, Miss de Clifford was powerfully drawn to cats, and she left her mark on Cats Protection. When her name came up in conversation, the speaker uttered it in a tone of deference and awe.

Miss de Clifford had first suggested an operation for female cats to her vet in 1946. 'He hesitated and told me that he had done it for his own cat and it was just like a hysterectomy,' she told me much later. At her insistence, Cats Protection came out in favour of the new form of birth control, and this remarkable woman's idea had somehow filtered down to us in a small Berkshire village in the 1950s. I cannot imagine how. Perhaps we had a forward-thinking vet.

So we had our females fixed, but like everybody else, we believed in the myth that every female cat should have at least one litter for health reasons. When Simpkin became pregnant, the plan was for her kittens to be drowned by one of our farm workers. That was the traditional fate for unwanted kittens at the time. My mother, who was tender-hearted towards animals, insisted that one single kitten should be left. 'Simpkin must have one kitten to nurse,' she argued. Thus Simpkin was given the chance to rear a son, Moppet. He was assigned to me, aged eight, as 'my' cat.

I loved him a lot, although I don't remember that he had any particular preference for me. His daughter Scrappy, begotten by him before his snip on a cat who lived in the village, was the smallest of the three white cats, and assigned to my younger brother. We three children may have thought we owned the cats, but they allowed no particular ownership.

In fact, Simpkin, Moppet and Scrappy led independent lives of their own, spending most of their time mousing in the farm buildings, coming in merely to eat and sleep. While the family dogs followed my father with adoring devotion wherever he went, the cats kept a sensible distance from him. In winter, however, they would sleep with whichever child had space on his or her bed. My bed was sometimes crowded with animals – two cats, carefully sleeping on different areas of the bed, inside or out, and often one of the three dogs if my father was not in the house that evening.

Cats can be playful but Moppet, Simpkin and Scrappy refused to play my childish games. I would take the fireguards, which were put round the open fires, into the garden and make them into a cage. The dogs would sit happily in my little private zoo. The cats, however often I placed them inside, would simply jump out immediately.

I used to dress up the family dogs occasionally. None of our three cats allowed this. Fancy dress was not a game that amused them. Nevertheless, those white cats, who accompanied me from the age of seven to 13, left their gentle paw marks on my heart. Moppet did more than that. He left an unhealed scar on my heart. His unhappy fate still makes me, some half a century later, want to cry. Moppet had the bad luck to fall foul of my father.

I loved my father but he frightened me. He didn't have much time for his second daughter. 'Women,' he would say in a voice loaded with scorn. 'Give them a place to put their handbag down and they will do any old boring job.' Having a second daughter, instead of the longed-for son, was not what he wanted. I was surplus to requirements.

I felt he despised me. If I cried about anything, he would jeer, 'I'll hang two jam jars round your neck to see which fills up first.' My sister and brother were brave. I wasn't. 'You're the coward of the family,' he would say to me. He hated weakness of any kind. In my first six or seven years of life I was often ill and was several times in hospital. 'You're the runt of the litter,' he would say.

No wonder then that I felt particularly sorry for the real runt of the litter in our pig sty near the stables. Sensible farmers keep the best piglets, not the runt, for breeding. The runt goes for slaughter. It is not fit to breed from. I would scrounge unwanted food from the kitchen, hoping to feed Hoggie, as I named her. I have a photograph of myself, wearing dungarees, crouched in the sty with piglets milling around me, as I tried to make sure she got the food. I hoped to fatten her, so that she would be rescued from slaughter and might be kept for breeding. I couldn't save her.

However, the 'runt of the litter' struck deep into my heart. My father's careless classification of me meant that I identified with unwanted animals, and felt the need to rescue them. I have wondered if that phrase may also play a part in why I have never had children or felt fit to be a mother. As unloved children, and some unhappy adults, often do, I tried to give the animals around me the love and the help that I needed. The seeds of my decision to rescue Tilly had been sown and nurtured in my own childhood. For 18 months she had been unwanted and unadopted. At a deep level, I knew a little of what it felt like.

My father tolerated the family cats. He appreciated their role as pest controllers. The cats, the farm and his family were ruled by him. His careless good nature was interspersed with savage rage. His body language was that of physical ease. His character was more complex. He was an alpha male, no doubt about that. I was in fear of him as were several of his workers.

His good points were an abounding energy, enthusiasm, enjoyment of food and fun, and an inquiring if totally undisciplined mind. He was fearless. The business of his life was fox hunting, plus occasional stag and otter hunting. If fox hunting was not available, he would go stalking in Scotland, or pheasant shooting. In general, if it was a nice day, he went out and killed something. Like the cats, really. While he may have had some respect for the hunting prowess of cats, animals were things he used and owned. I think he may have loved his dogs, although love was an emotion he rarely showed. He may have cared for one or two of his horses. Mostly, he just rode them.

He would punish animals without a second thought, beating the horses round the head if their behaviour offended him, and hitting the dogs. He had, he said, been beaten regularly as a young child at prep school and later, so he was only doing to animals what had been done to him. Such is the cycle of abuse.

People who knew him well tell me he loved me. Now, as an adult, I realize he did. To me, as a nervous child, this seemed unlikely. His feeling for me was, I thought, mostly contempt. He was not a man to cross. He did not do forgiveness. In his eighties, when he faced death, courageously and without complaint or self-pity, I asked him if he wanted to see a cousin with whom he had quarrelled. He said, 'I haven't forgiven him.'

Moppet fell foul of his rage. 'That bloody cat!' stormed my father as he strode into the farmhouse kitchen. 'He's killed one of my pigeons. I'll make him pay for it. He won't do it again after I've finished with him.'

My father's prized nun pigeons, white with black heads and tails, lived in a cote built into one of the barns. My father had caught Moppet with a dead pigeon in his mouth. The fact that cats in general instinctively kill birds, and all three of ours occasionally caught them, did not save Moppet from punishment. He had killed something belonging to my father. He must suffer.

The punishment was a dreadful one. The dead pigeon was soaked in paraffin and tied tightly around poor Moppet's neck. Anybody who has put a collar on a cat knows how distressed they can become when an ordinary one is put on them for the fist time. Poor Moppet, yoked to a hideously smelling corpse, dragged himself and the dead pigeon round the farmyard in misery and terror. Neither I nor my mother dared to intervene on his behalf.

'Come upstairs,' said my mother quietly to me the following morning when my father was safely out on the farm and there was nobody to overhear us. 'I've got something to show you. You needn't worry about Moppet any more. He's all right. I've rescued him.'

She took me up to the spare bedroom, a room full of junk at the back of the house where nobody went. Moppet lay exhausted on a blanket in a cardboard box. His fur was soaked in paraffin and he was valiantly trying to lick it off. My mother had searched the farmyard and found him huddled, still tied to the corpse, in one of the barns. She had cut the pigeon off his bruised neck and hidden him in the spare room where he could recover from his ordeal without my father knowing.

It broke him. From that moment on, Moppet lived in a state of chronic anxiety. He stopped taking proper care of his coat and began to look manky and dirty. He started peeing in the house in a desperate attempt to make himself feel better by marking his territory. Not long afterwards, he was run over on the busy main road that ran alongside our garden wall.

My father took me to see the corpse. 'Come on. You'd better see what's happened,' he said to me. Moppet's limp body lay just outside the garden gate. Perhaps with his last remaining strength he had been trying to crawl home.

My father wanted me to see the body. He believed in toughening up children, ready for hard times in later life. As a male child, I would have been expected to enjoy killing animals for sport, as he did. Females, fortunately, didn't have to shoot animals, only hunt them. I had already shown terror on my pony, and had refused to go fox hunting. Since I was clearly the coward of the family, he may have thought I needed extra toughening.

Seeing Moppet's corpse didn't harden my heart. Instead it came as a warning to me. I felt I was living in a household that would never be truly safe. I must take care to tread more carefully than poor Moppet had done. I dealt with my father by avoiding him as much as possible and by abject grovelling to his authority.

'I'll leave my mark on you, Celia,' my father often used to say, glaring down at me from his place at the head of the dining table as we ate our meals. 'You may not like it. You may try to escape it, but my mark will stay with you forever.'

He has indeed marked me forever, although not in the way he thought he had. I saw the way he beat horses when they did not do what he wanted. I saw the way he saved money by getting his cows treated by a cow doctor who cut off their horns without anaesthetic so that the yard was full of their bleeding, mooing distress. As an adult, I understand that this cruelty stemmed from his intense unhappiness. He was locked into an unhappy marriage. He had been beaten and abused as a child. It had left him abnormally sensitive to any kind of slight or insult, unable to deal with disagreements except by rage, and with the ability to shut off pain, whether his or someone else's. In later life, and in a happy second marriage, he became more contented and thus kinder to animals. As a child, however, I could not understand these subtleties; I just identified with his victims.

He left his mark on me, as he had promised he would. But he softened me rather than hardened me. Identification with abused animals has marked me for all of my life. It is difficult for me to separate myself from the wounded, starved, abused and unhappy animals in our society. I can pretend they are not there. I can ignore them if I am busy enough, drunk enough or just in denial. But more often I feel as if part of me suffers with them, particularly if I actually witness their pain – which is why I felt the distress of the small tortoiseshell cat cowering in Ann's rescue pen.

My childhood left me with a need to be close to animals, but this wasn't always a good thing for the animals concerned. I have not always been a responsible owner. I got into trouble at boarding school for keeping a white mouse surreptitiously in my bedroom locker. Another white mouse spent time with me at Cambridge University, until, aware that my boyfriend was taking up too much of my time, I gave her and her cage away to somebody who wanted her.

When I first arrived in London in the Swinging Sixties, I was given a kitten, a Burmese I named Tunku. He simply disappeared one day when he felt old enough to go. Mine was a lifestyle unsuitable for pet keeping. I lived in a mews house with two other tenants. I played loud music. Boyfriends were always coming and going, as I seemed unable to lead a sensible sex life. I drank too much, wore mini skirts and high boots, went to nightclubs patronised by pop stars, including Mick Jagger, and often returned home in the early hours. Tunku very sensibly left home, as cats do if they feel their home is uncongenial.

My next pet was Jelly, a charming mongrel who joined me in my first marriage. I used to take him for a walk first thing before leaving for work. When my marriage broke up, I took Jelly with me. As I moved poor Jelly to various carers, it became clear that I couldn't keep him properly. So I advertised and found a home for him. I was learning – slowly – to be more responsible for the welfare of my animals.

So far I had tried having a pet, and the experience had shown me that I wasn't good at it. I had begun as the typical irresponsible pet keeper – acquiring animals then failing to care for them properly. I didn't want to be that kind of person any more, so I decided I could not have a pet. If you truly love animals, you may not be able to have one of your own.

So for many years I would not let myself have a pet. I was working hard in Fleet Street, often coming home late at night. Then I remarried. My second husband, Ronnie, didn't want animals, either. As a hot-shot foreign correspondent and war reporter, he often had to jump on a plane at very short notice indeed. I would come home to find a scrawled message waiting for me: 'Off to Cyprus for Turkish invasion. Love, Ronnie.'

I never intended to have a cat. And if Ada had not arrived in my life, I would never have had one. However, she decided that the shed at the bottom of my small London garden was the ideal place to have her kitten. Why she chose the shed, I do not know. Perhaps because I did so little gardening!

At first, I thought two cats were living there, because I would see her sitting outside the shed in the company of a bigger black tom cat. The black tom came and went but she remained in the garden, close to the shed. Finally, when I investigated, I found a single kitten in an empty cardboard box that she had chosen. She had pulled out her own fur to line the box as a nest.

I moved her and the kitten into the house. Her arrival coincided with my leaving an office job and freelancing from home, so keeping a cat was now a possibility. I told my husband that this was a temporary measure, 'just till I can find them a good home,' and we named the kitten Billy Fury, because of his wild temperament.

Ada was a good mother – far too good a mother. She had decided that Billy should be educated as a feral, not as a pet. She taught him how to hide by climbing behind the drainpipes underneath the kitchen sink. He could not be extracted from there by a human hand, and nor could the tiny space be easily blocked off. If I came anywhere near the kitchen, Ada would chirrup, sending him back into this sanctuary.

For a week or so I tried to tame him but to little avail. His mother was teaching him to avoid all humans. If he started moving towards me, she would call him back immediately. I needed to get him away from her, but finding a home for him was difficult.

In those days many of the local animal rescue charities put down a huge proportion of the cats handed in. Any cat of an unpopular colour or unfriendly temperament would be euthanized. I feared that might happen to poor Billy. I didn't reckon his chances were good.

The local pet shop said they would take him for sale but I didn't want to see a living creature just handed over the counter like a tin of cat food. I put up notices in all the local newsagents and small shops and eventually found somebody willing to adopt him. I handed him over with a bag of food and litter.

I hope that he was young enough to adapt to domestic life. If I'd known then what I know now, I would have made sure I socialized him properly, that is to say, made him familiar with humans and a human home. But I didn't know that is what I should have done. My instinct to take him into the kitchen and out of the shed was correct, but by not handling him enough in his early life, I had put his future happiness as a pet at risk. I feel bad about it still.

Ada remained in my house, wanted by me but unwanted by Ronnie. She didn't seem to like him, or indeed any men at all, and he found this hurtful. She was particularly scared if he came home after a few drinks with the boys at the end of a Fleet Street day. She could tell his state of inebriation from his footsteps up our small London street. She would suddenly disappear from the living room before he reached the front door.

He came home one night in a bad mood. I was on the floor, communing with Ada. She was sitting underneath the windowsill and I was talking to her as if she was human. Despite the fact that I had halved the feline population in our home by getting the kitten adopted, Ronnie was not in the mood to find my preoccupation with a cat either funny or pleasing.

'That damn cat ... why haven't you found her a home? I tell you, Celia, if that cat doesn't go, I will,' he declared.

I respond to authority either with aggression or with outright deceit. I wanted to say to Ronnie, 'You go, then,' but this was clearly a time for dishonesty. So I choked back the desire to tell him that he, rather than Ada, could leave home, and instead lied.

'I am desperately looking for a home for her, Ronnie. Just give it a few more weeks,' I said mildly.

She stayed, of course.

For the next month or so I told Ronnie repeatedly how hard I was looking for a home for Ada. I itemized all the people who had told me they didn't want a cat. I reported how the various rescue charities would probably have to put her down because she was nervous and unattractive – sadly true. I begged for more time and for his understanding. Ronnie is a kind man with a gentle heart. His threat to leave home if I kept her had been merely the passing irritation of a man who has had a bad day. I was betting that his kindness would overcome his reluctance to become a cat owner.

It worked. A few months later he accepted the fact that I had a cat. Then he accepted that *we* had a cat.

Ada was my education in things feline. I knew nothing when she and I first met. I did not plan to have a cat until she moved into my life. I hadn't chosen her; she had chosen me. First I liked her, then I loved her, then I adored her.

After Ada's arrival, I was completely and utterly under the spell of cats.

Chapter 3

Big Boomer, my first foster cat

Tilly's arrival in my home was not promising. I had taken my cat carrier to Ann, and was expecting that we would gently lift her into it.

'She'll never go into one of those,' said Ann. 'The only way to get her in a carrier is to use one that opens up from the top. I'd better do it. She's used to me.'

With the skill of somebody who has handled many a difficult cat, Ann cornered Tilly in the cat pen and popped her into one of her own carriers. We put the lid down on the trembling Tilly and I carried her to my car. She stayed silent as I drove home.

I had prepared the spare room as a cat residence. There was a litter tray, with the large wooden litter pellets used by Cats Protection. A familiar type of litter made it more likely that Tilly would be happy to use the tray. There was food and there was water. I opened the cat carrier and Tilly shot out of it and ran under the bed.

She hid there, quivering, backed up against the wall at the far end, as far away from me as possible. To see her at all I had to lie down flat on my stomach. I knew that cats are often frightened in new territory and the kindest thing you can do is just shut them in a room and leave them alone. So I shut the door and left her.

I wasn't to see her again for days.

Her behaviour was strikingly different from that of my only previous foster cat, Boomer. Six months earlier I had prepared the same room in the same way for Boomer. When I opened *his* cat carrier, he had strolled slowly out, looked carefully around, and with an effort leaped on, not under, the bed.

Boomer was my first foster cat. I had said I would occasionally foster cats for Cats Protection, about a month after our previous cat William's death. I was busy studying and had decided to put off having another cat for a while.

'No cat could ever replace William,' Ronnie had said firmly. Ronnie, the man who claimed to enjoy a 'cat-free ambience', had been very upset by William's death. It seemed to him almost disrespectful just to get another cat. It would be like trying to replace the irreplaceable. William, with his long-haired beauty and gentle nature, had been the feline love of Ronnie's life. Ronnie needed some time to mourn before we – or I – brought another cat home.

Fostering was a solution that would give me some cats in my life in the meantime. Fostering a cat is not as much of a commitment as adoption. The cat is owned by the charity and stays with the fosterer while waiting for a new home to be found. Our little branch of Cats Protection has a devoted band of volunteers who are fosterers. Most people think that rescue organizations have miles of dog kennels and cattery pens on one site. In our charity, this isn't so. There *are* regional adoption centres in Cats Protection, but much of the rescue work in small branches consists of fostering by individuals.

'Can you take in a cat urgently?' asked Olivia, the local Cats Protection welfare officer. It was just a few days before Christmas. 'I can't find anybody else. He's one of ours.'

Olivia lived and breathed cats so she had looked up Boomer in the records when she got a call about him. Boomer been adopted a year earlier as an indoor-only cat by an elderly man who lived on his own. Mr Barton (not his real name) was finding Boomer too difficult to manage. Boomer had apparently been trying to dash out of the house each time the front door was opened and the elderly man had almost tripped over him several times.

'Mr Barton is going to his daughter's for Christmas,' explained Olivia. 'She thinks it's best if the cat is out of the house before he comes home. She feels this is the kindest way to part her father from the cat. He just can't manage him any more.'

Ronnie and I don't do elaborate celebrations over Christmas so the house was going to be fairly quiet. A temporary cat would be no trouble. Normally, Cats Protection will neither take in nor give out cats over the Christmas period. This is to stop people taking away cats as Christmas presents. Boomer, however, was an emergency.

It was snowing when we set off to collect him from a small house in one of the Thames valley villages below the Cotswold Hills. The street lights lit up a winter scene that was like a Christmas card. Thatched roofs, unlike the more common tiled ones, were sprinkled with snow. Smoke from wood fires rose from the chimneys, and sparkling Christmas trees and decorations could be seen through lighted windows with curtains undrawn.

As instructed by Olivia, I went to the house next to Mr Barton's and knocked on the door of the neighbour who was feeding Boomer in his owner's absence. She was expecting me.

'Thank goodness you're here,' she said. 'That cat has really got too much for Mr B. It's going to cause him a terrible fall one of these days. He's so unsteady on his feet. He's no longer safe to have a cat like this one.'

She opened the door for me and I went in with my carrier, armed with a pocketful of cat treats. Straight in front of us was a staircase leading up to the bedrooms. On it sat a huge white-and-black cat. In shape, he looked like a very big furry pear. His head was normal sized but the body below it sort of overflowed on to the carpet. He was so large that he couldn't fit on a single stair. So his back half was on one stair and his front half was on the stair below.

'Yes, he is big,' said the neighbour apologetically when she saw my reaction. 'That's one of the difficulties.'

Boomer would have been the fattest cat I had ever seen, but for the fact that I had met the legendary Tiddles, the cat who lived in London's Paddington station ladies lavatory in the 1970s. If Boomer was gigantic, Tiddles was super-gigantic.

Tiddles had turned up at the station as a six-week-old tabby-and-white kitten in 1970 and had been adopted by the whole staff of the ladies lavatory. In those days before health and hygiene bureaucracy, the stationmaster gave permission for Tiddles to live in the loo full time and he became a prime attraction to all females using the toilets. Postcards and food parcels were sent to him from as far away as Hong Kong and New York.

Alas, the food parcels did him nothing but harm. As a feline celebrity he was already being fed by every single one of the staff. His tummy became so saggy that his upper legs disappeared into it. His whole body was bursting with fat, and his head and his tail looked tiny in proportion to the vast torso between them. By 1982, he weighed about 14.5 kg (32 lb) and was hitting the record books. Surprisingly, he lived until the age of 13, more or less a normal lifespan for a pet cat.

My encounter with Tiddles had played a part in turning me over to the dark side, as cat haters would see it. Until then I had not been particularly interested in animals as a subject for journalism. I was working for the *Sunday Times Magazine* at the time and had complained to the editor, 'Everybody else has a title. I don't.' As an office joke I was given the title of 'pets editor' and, to everybody's surprise, I started living up to the role. Tiddles was the subject of my very first article on companion animals, which is the posh term for pets.

Boomer, the white-and-black cat that now sat gazing down on me from the staircase was smaller than the legendary Tiddles, being a mere 8 kg (17½ lb). I looked at him and wondered if I dare just walk up the stairs and pick him up. Did I have the strength? Would he let me? Or would he bolt back into the bedrooms. It seemed unwise to try. I turned to the neighbour.

'Do you think if I put out some food for him in the kitchen he would come down?' I asked her.

'I should think so. He never stops eating,' she said. I put a few cat treats on the floor at the bottom of the stairs. Boomer came waddling down and ate them with relish.

I laid a trail of treats towards the cat carrier on the kitchen floor. Obligingly, Boomer followed it and, just as he was hoovering up the last treat close to the carrier, I knelt down, with my knees either side of him, and pushed him in. He just about fitted inside. If I had known how bulky he was, I would have brought a bigger carrier.

'Give me some of his food to take home,' I said to the neighbour. My idea was to lift Boomer in his carrier with one hand and the food in the other, but when I tried to lift the carrier, I realized I couldn't manage both. So the neighbour followed behind me with the bag of food. On the snow-covered slippery street the carrier felt as if it weighed a ton. I heaved it into the backseat of the car, said goodbye to the neighbour and took Boomer home.

He seemed unworried about being uprooted from his old home, when I let him out into my spare room. After about five minutes sitting on top of the bed, he jumped off, walked to the food bowl and ate all the food I had left there ready for him. Then he heaved himself back on the bed and made himself comfortable at the pillow end for a nap. It was clear that in Boomer's world, food came before anything else.

His food obsession had been one reason why Boomer had come back into Cats Protection's care. His owner had been far too generous with the food bowl. Originally, Boomer had been rescued by the RSPCA from a household full of cats. Apparently, he had jumped out of the window into the arms of the RSPCA inspector. Luckily, at that stage he was average sized; otherwise, she would have been knocked unconscious by this feline missile.

Normally, he would have been neutered, cleaned up and rehomed by the RSPCA. Alas for Boomer, he tested positive for FIV, Feline Immunodeficiency Virus, a disease similar to HIV in humans. The local RSPCA inspector passed him to our Cats Protection branch, thinking we would probably find a home for him more easily than the RSPCA branch could.

At the time of his first rescue, Boomer was about three years old, still healthy and not at all fat. However, he was an FIV carrier and, although he could not pass on the disease to humans, he could pass it on to other cats. So he needed a home as an indoor-only pet. An indoor life would be restrictive for him, but it was his only alternative to euthanasia. He had been adopted by Mr Barton and, in theory, there was no reason why this shouldn't have worked out well. Boomer's lifespan might not be the full 14 years or so, but as his new owner was in his eighties this probably didn't matter.

Boomer's behaviour, however, had ruined the relationship. He had the habit of digging in his litter tray as if he was trying to tunnel to Australia. Litter would fly into the air for several feet. Only after about four minutes of heavy digging would he use the tray. Mr Barton was finding it difficult to clean up not just the tray but all the litter that was scattered over the kitchen.

Boomer also begged for food on all possible occasions – and his kindly old owner could not bear to refuse him. So his weight ballooned. His frequent attempts to escape by the front door were becoming ever more dangerous as his bulk increased – 3.5 kg (8 lb) of normal-sized cat dashing towards the front door risked toppling his owner; 8 kg (17½ lb) of very fat cat pushing his way out was even more dangerous. Boomer had become a feline tank.

'He'll have to be slimmed down,' I said to Ronnie the evening of his arrival. 'I'd better not give him too much food tonight.'

'Don't be so mean to the poor chap,' Ronnie objected. 'Let him have his grub. It's Christmas.'

Ronnie, despite being less fond of cats than I am, has always partly identified with the felines in our house. He likes his food and does not approve of dieting. He likes cats who like food. Feline castration in particular worries him. He goes quiet and thoughtful if it's mentioned. In William's case, I'd had to book the surgical procedure without telling Ronnie the date. Luckily for Ronnie, Boomer had already been fixed.

The next day Boomer took an exploratory walk downstairs to the kitchen, probably to see if there was any food there. He had used his litter tray and the whole spare room was scattered with litter. I found an elongated very large cardboard box that I laid on its side. If I placed the litter tray in it as far back as possible, most of the flying litter stayed inside the box.

Doing something about Boomer's size was not going to be so easy. He was a very sociable cat and on the second evening came downstairs to sit beside me on the sofa. He did not try to get on my lap, which was just as well as he would not have fitted on to it.

Fat cats, for some reason, make people laugh, and I'm afraid I laughed at Boomer that evening, until I took a closer look at him. He was a short-haired cat about four years old with bright eyes and clean-looking ears. His coat was another matter.

His backside had numerous mats where the hair had knotted. There were also bits of dried poo. He had smaller mats at the top of his tail along his back. Cats are clean creatures and will normally groom the hair all over their body so that mats do not form. Obviously, Boomer had not been doing this. Poo and mats on the backside were a sign that something was wrong.

Then the simple fact dawned on me. Boomer's bottom was dirty because he was just too fat to reach it. He was also unable to twist and reach the far end of his back where the little mats were forming. For him, being a fat cat was no joke. In the short term he needed help to clean himself up, and in the long term he must definitely lose weight for his own sake.

The next day when my nephew came for Christmas, I told him, 'I have a job for you.' Jess is the devoted owner of a very large British Blue pedigree feline called Herbie. British Blues are heavy cats and Herbie is also fat. He weighs almost as much as Boomer did. Jess was therefore the ideal person to help me handle this weighty cat.

'Wow. He is big. He's bigger than Herbie,' Jess said appreciatively, when we went up to Boomer's spare room after Christmas lunch. I had shut Boomer away from the celebrations, quiet though they were. I could see from Jess's expression that finding a cat fatter than Herbie was an agreeable surprise.

'Can you feel his ribs at all?' I asked him. I couldn't.

'No, I can't,' confirmed Jess. Boomer's ribs were cushioned so thickly with fat that they had all but disappeared. His tummy on the other hand had expanded. It reached halfway down to the floor. It was not a saggy tummy. It was too tightly full of fat to sag. Something had to be done.

Jess held Boomer as I used scissors to cut off the biggish mats on his backside and the smaller ones on the upper part of his back. I then cleaned his backside with a soapy flannel, which he did not enjoy. When it was over, however, he shook himself and looked relieved before settling down for another nap.

Dieting Boomer took some thought. If I were simply to starve him, he might develop fatty liver disease, *hepatic lipidosis*, when the liver of a fat cat collapses under the stress of too little food. I reckoned I needed a vet's advice before starting Operation Fit Not Fat for Boomer. The snow was falling and it looked as if we might be snowed in. A good neighbour, Jonathon, who had a Landrover with four-wheel drive, was kind enough to take me to Boomer's local vet.

As we drove through the now heavy snow, I could see from Jonathon's expression that all this seemed a lot of fuss for a fat cat. He and his wife Susie are not cat lovers and Susie has been known to say, 'Money spent on all that cat food at the supermarkets could feed thousands of starving Africans.' But Jonathon knew it mattered to me and if it mattered to me, he would help.

The vet on duty weighed Boomer on some baby scales. (These suit cats nicely and this inspired me to buy my own.) Then she prescribed a special slimming diet and, most important of all, the plastic measuring device to make sure I didn't give him too much or too little food.

'I think he's got a heart murmur,' she remarked finally, while checking him with a stethoscope. 'Yes he has.' This may have played a part in Boomer's lethargy and thus his weight gain. I was glad I had bothered to have him checked out before starting the diet. She gave me medication for his heart problem.

Dieting cats is difficult for people who love them to distraction. It is so easy to give in to their pleading for food. Boomer was not my cat, so I reckoned I would be able to do it. I didn't have to feel that tangle of guilt and shame that afflicts the owners of fat cats. I was not the one who had let him get into this huge and unhappy state.

Every day, I simply measured out the correct amount (according to his weight) and put it in a jam jar to be fed to him throughout the day. Whatever happened, Boomer never ever got anything more than what was in the jam jar.

Naturally, he went into pleading mode. He was good at giving me plaintive and unhappy looks. The occasional tiny kitten mew – odd coming from so large a body – was part of his pleading routine. His body language told me that I was a hard-hearted woman, depriving him of everything he wanted in life. After eating the small portion I put down for his breakfast, he would trail round after me, looking upset.

Cats can be as good at begging for food as dogs are. Boomer had honed his methods well during his year with the old gentleman – it was his successful food pleading that had allowed him to accumulate all that fat –and after a while, it began to get to me. I started feeling guilty. I had to have a strategy that would help me withstand him. Just saying 'No' was becoming increasingly difficult.

'Fun not food,' I declared to Ronnie one morning. 'I've got it. The Celia Haddon diet for cats will substitute fun for food. That way I don't have to feel so hard-hearted.'

My aim was to respond positively not negatively to Boomer's pleading looks. When he asked for food, I would respond by offering a game with a piece of string or throw him a wine cork to chase. Fun not food. That way, I would feel less mean.

Exercise, now that he had medication for his heart murmur, would help him lose weight. Fat cats find it an effort to move at all. Just offering games with string might not be enough. Boomer needed to be motivated into more activity.

The obvious incentive was food. He was so food obsessed that he would do anything to get it. Two days after that visit to the vet, I got rid of his food bowl altogether. He was no longer going to get his food given to him on a plate, so to speak. He would have to earn it by joining a gym!

I designed a kind of circuit for him by putting one or two cat biscuits in several carefully chosen places – on the living-room windowsills, at the top of his climbing frame, on his sleeping spot on the sofa and on the armchair. At breakfast time he would gallop from place to place while I would be two or three places ahead of him, putting down biscuits on the surfaces he had already eaten from. Boomer showed signs of greatly enjoying the process.

After he began to lose a little weight, I made it more complicated. In addition to the food circuit, I started feeding him in home-made food puzzles. I cut a large hole in the middle of the box from the chocolates given to me at Christmas. The hole had to be big so that his head would not get stuck inside. I would put a biscuit or two inside the box, so that he had to hook them out with his paw. I also cut holes in a lavatory inner roll, stopped it at both ends with brown sticky tape and inserted cat biscuits into it. To get to them he had to roll the device over the floor until the biscuits fell out. I made a similar feeding device from a small plastic bottle.

Later, as he slimmed down further, I added one or two cardboard boxes to the circuit. To get the food inside, he had to leap right inside each box. Each morning, midday and evening, we both went into a kind of frenzy – me putting cat biscuits down in about ten different places, and Boomer a few seconds behind me getting them out and eating them.

We both enjoyed the race. I laughed a lot seeing his tubby bottom disappearing into the boxes. He whisked around, his body language showing that he liked the action, not just the food reward. An indoor cat such as Boomer didn't have much in his life. There were no mice to hunt, no hedgerows to patrol, and no interesting outside smells to investigate. He was stuck inside all day. The feeding devices gave him a bit of fun. Hooking cat biscuits out of a chocolate box could not compete with mousing, but it was at least some kind of activity.

At first, although Boomer was losing weight according to my baby scales, he did not look much slimmer. The first visible sign of success came after a couple of weeks on this regime. I saw him sitting back on his haunches and cleaning his tummy. He looked ridiculous sitting with his legs akimbo and a huge tummy billowing out. But he also looked happy. He could actually reach his backside for the first time.

From that moment on, Boomer groomed and groomed and groomed himself devotedly every day to make up for the time that he'd had to live in unclean fur. He spent many hours washing every part of himself with evident enjoyment. Cats need to wash like dogs need to chew. It makes them feel good. A cat who cannot groom is a cat deprived of an important source of pleasure and wellbeing. Boomer felt better.

He was an endearing cat. Naturally, being a cat on a diet, he spent a lot of time in the kitchen. He would forage around the kitchen floor like a hunting dog, seeking out any small fragment of food that had fallen down. Despite his bulk, he managed to jump on to the kitchen table and the kitchen surfaces in his relentless hunt for food. I learned to put all food of any kind away.

He also targeted Ronnie, the weakest link in the diet programme. I once came home to find Boomer sitting about two inches from Ronnie's plate, trying to intervene as Ronnie's food travelled on his fork to his mouth. He didn't quite dare to hook it off with his paw but you could see that he was considering this daring move. Ronnie was admiring his persistence and dropping the odd bit of food from his fork.

Despite being strictly dieted, I think Boomer enjoyed his stay with us. He would sleep companionably next to me on the sofa. At night, if I spent time in the spare room as I sometimes did, he would insert himself carefully on the bed between my back and the wall. He was a big cat but he had learned to make the best of the space available and once in place, he never stirred at all throughout the night. He was a good sleeping partner, despite his bulk.

In one way, he still presented a major problem. Boomer was desperate to get to the great outdoors. Our house is up a cart track among the cornfields and that winter the track was full of game birds, French partridges and pheasants. I also had a bird table to feed the garden birds during the cold weather. Boomer would sit on the windowsill and watch the wildlife. His head would be down and poking forwards in the typical position of a cat thinking of killing something.

I fed the game birds outside the living-room window for his amusement. At first, I thought this might provide a bit of fun for him, but as the weeks went on and nobody wanted to adopt a fat indoor cat, I began to sense his growing frustration. Watching the partridges from his windowsill just made his life as an indoor cat more difficult for him. Finally, he made a break for it. I had locked the cat flap but Boomer hurled himself at it with such force that he broke right through the plastic.

'He's done a runner,' Ronnie yelled up to me in my upstairs office. 'It's the great escape.'

I ran downstairs to see Boomer joyfully disporting himself in the garden. I have a photo taken just before he plunged into the bushes for a wonderful afternoon's hunting. We didn't see him for three hours. I walked round calling 'Boomer' to no avail. He was making the most of his freedom.

It was the rattle of the food bag later in the day that got him in again and, for once, I let him have more than his usual portion. After that glorious escape, I nailed a wooden plank against the cat flap and he never got out again. I stopped feeding the pheasants close to the windowsill so that he would not feel so frustrated at being kept indoors.

I had thought about adopting him but I realized that, if I did, I would not have the heart to keep him indoors all his life. Yet, if I let him out, his FIV status would make him a danger to my neighbour's elegant Siamese, Miss Ruby Fou. In any case, I would be allowed to adopt him only if I promised to keep him as an indoor cat. I felt he would be miserable living where he could see, but not touch, the wildlife outside.

So Boomer had to stay my foster cat and I had to be willing to give him up to somebody else. He wasn't going to be an easy cat to place in a home. True, he was white and black, rather than black and white, not such a bad colour. He was also affectionate and confident round humans, and since people find fat cats funny, his weight was probably not such a drawback. Besides, after three months with me he had lost 1.5 kg (3¼ lb), weighing in at a more reasonable 6.5 kg (14¼ lb). It was his FIV status that would put off a lot of would-be adopters. People are frightened that FIV might spread to humans, even though there is no recorded instance of this happening.

I had to think of a way to help him find a home. I started to teach him little tricks – sitting on command, shaking hands, leaping over an obstacle and sitting up on his haunches in the traditional dog begging pose.

Being a cat focused on food, he learned very quickly indeed that the correct behaviour produced a cat biscuit. Now we could put him on the Cats Protection website as a cat who did tricks – it did the trick for him. He found somebody to adopt him.

Boomer went home with a lovely woman called Marianne who lived in a flat isolated by stairs from the front door of the block. He would not be able to get out and, better still, he would not be frustrated by the sight of too much wildlife. I knew this would be a better home for him than I could give him.

I let him go with a heavy heart. After three months I had become very attached to him. I handed over his diet food and the measuring cup, and squeezed him into the rather small carrier his new owner had brought with her. Off he went down the track in her car and I never saw him again.

Several months later I heard from Marianne. She emailed me to say: 'I meant to email you earlier to tell you that Boomer still does his tricks and he is still on his diet. I am late in emailing because shortly after seeing you I got a diagnosis of cancer. I would never have managed to go through it all without Boomer's support.'

I wanted to cry when I read these touching words. Was it a kind of foreboding?

Chapter 4

The invisible cat

Looking at the glaring eyes, huddled body and fluffed-up, staring coat of the cat under the bed in my small spare room, it was clear that Tilly was not going to be as easy a foster cat as Boomer had been. Laughter and affection is what Boomer and I had shared. Neither looked attainable with Tilly. She cringed as far away from me as possible and was frozen into immobility. Really frightened animals either flee, fight or freeze. She froze.

That first night in the spare room Tilly neither ate the food I had left out for her nor used the litter tray. This was extremely worrying. I am not house proud but neither am I fond of the smell of cat urine on the carpet. This little brown cat was clearly very disturbed indeed. Was she doing it under the bed? I couldn't smell anything so I didn't try to move the bed for a better look.

Ronnie was still in hospital and already unenthusiastic about the new feline lodger. 'I want a kitten,' he grumbled each time the subject came up. 'I don't want the cat that nobody else wants. I want a *nice* cat.'

I had hoped that I might succeed in luring Tilly out from under the bed before he came home. After all, Boomer had settled in and explored after only two or three days. It would have been great if Tilly had behaved in a similar fashion. This hope now looked completely unrealistic.

When I looked in the next morning, before leaving to visit Ronnie in hospital, my heart sank as I saw that the litter tray was still unused. I left her in the room with the door shut. Wide-open spaces frighten nervous cats. Besides, if she was going be unreliable in using the litter tray, I preferred accidents to happen in the spare room where the carpet was particularly old.

'How's that ugly cat doing?' he asked me when I arrived in hospital for my daily visit.

'Oh, it's all right. She's still rather nervous, of course,' I lied. I was reluctant to tell him the full truth yet.

My worries about her increased when I got back from hospital. Her food was untouched. So was the litter tray.

I knew that cats could retain their urine for about 36 hours, if they were really desperate not to pee. Possibly she was just too terrified in her new surroundings to venture out at all. Would she just do it under the bed? If that happened, she would have to go back to Ann and return to the cat pen.

Ronnie was reluctant to have an ugly, frightened cat in the house but he would surely draw the line at a cat who was ugly, frightened *and* incontinent. And I wasn't sure that even I, the cat lover of the household, could bear to clean up cat pee from the carpet every morning. I love cats, but I didn't think I loved them that much.

I rang up Ann to ask about Tilly's litter tray use in the cat pen. 'Neither of the cats knew what a litter tray was at first,' she told me, 'but they settled down. There were no problems after that.'

The following morning was eureka day. I looked in and saw she had eaten her food and used the litter tray during the night. If you foster cats in your home, the moment when they start using the litter tray is a moment of joyful relief. No messes to clear up. No worries about the carpet.

She had been holding back out of sheer terror. Maybe the poor little thing had never been properly domesticated. Perhaps I had a wild animal in my house and I must adjust my behaviour accordingly. It certainly seemed that Tilly had not come from a normal home. All I had been told about her was that she and Lottie had been handed in from a smallholding where there were too many cats, both inside and outside the house.

On day four she was still huddled by the back wall under the bed. As far as I could tell she had not even explored the small spare room. When I looked around there was no trace of her, not even a single cat hair, on top of the bed, the soft surface where she might be expected to sleep. There was no sign that she had jumped on the windowsill to look out, as Boomer had done early on in his stay with me. She seemed to be coming out to eat and use the litter tray, then retreating immediately. Before she arrived I had installed a Feliway® Diffuser, a plug-in device that exudes a calming scent for felines. It did not seem to be doing much for her yet.

In theory, one way to reduce fear in an animal is to slowly let it get used to, and grow confident around, what it fears. So if a cat is frightened of people, you stay at a 'safe' distance till the cat relaxes, then move a tiny bit nearer. You can also make the cat feel good about your presence by giving it the chance to eat tasty treats when you are nearby. The idea is that the cat begins to associate you, the human, with the pleasure of food.

In a first trial of this, I lay on my stomach, lifted the bedspread and peered under the bed. I could see Tilly's terrified little body pressed against the back wall. There wasn't room under the bed for her to do anything but crouch motionless. I experimented by rolling a few cat treats towards her. She shrank back, pressing herself more tightly against the wall.

When I looked the following day, the cat treats were still there. In her mind, they had been contaminated by the fact that this frightening human had touched them. Winning her goodwill by means of food was not going to work at this stage. Indeed, so far, my scientific project to help turn her into an adoptable pet was a total failure. I would have to think again.

For the time being, I decided to stop all attempts to build a relationship. I kept the door closed so that she could feel safely shut away from me. I didn't look at her. I didn't try to make nice little noises at her. I didn't roll any more cat treats. I just went in twice a day to clean the litter tray and put down fresh water and food, as far away from the litter tray as possible. As she was still refusing to come out at all during the day, the evening visit was pretty unnecessary since both bowls and litter tray were untouched. But I went in to check all was well.

Thus began a long period of cat invisibility.

Ronnie was still dangerously ill, so I was focused on spending time with him, not her. Most of the day the house was very quiet. In the evening, when I got back from the hospital, I would microwave myself an instant meal, and sit watching TV. Our living room was just below Tilly's room, so, if nothing else, she was getting used to the distant sound of TV, something she did not have in the Cats Protection pen.

I did take time to look at her veterinary records during these first days. They revealed that she had been a very sick cat at the time she was handed over to Cats Protection. She was about four months old when she arrived on 10 January 2009, just before a spell of severe weather. The timing was lucky for her. She might well not have survived the winter snow and ice.

Her coat was dull and her tummy distended, said the records. She had worms and fleas and was not litter trained. 'She was so scruffy, I didn't even know she was long haired,' Ann told me. Eighteen months of good food and warm shelter in a Cats

Protection pen had helped her regain her health before she arrived in my home. She had not, however, grown much. Some cats can double their weight and size late in life, after a poor start. Tilly, young as she was, had not done so.

Perhaps this was because she had been in such poor condition when she was rescued. For several months the vet had felt it unwise even to give her vaccinations. She suffered from bloody diarrhoea and tested positive for *campylobacter*, an infection that she had probably picked up from sick cats in the overcrowded smallholding.

It had taken a whole four months of treatment, and a large veterinary bill for our small branch of Cats Protection, before she tested clear of the infection and was well enough to be vaccinated. Luckily for her, she had not caught FIV, like poor Boomer.

A month after that, according to her records, she was finally well enough to be spayed. After the operation she had torn off, or somehow removed, her post-op buster collar, a protective cone-shaped device in plastic, which stops animals interfering with wounds while they heal. As her then fosterer Ann could not get anywhere near her, Tilly couldn't be given a painkilling injection nor could her buster collar be put on again. Clearly, this small cat had a talent for stubborn, independent behaviour.

If I had only read these records *before* taking her home, I would have discovered she needed top-up vaccinations. Had I foreseen this, I could have left her with Ann until they were done.

Instead, I faced having somehow to pull her out from under the bed and put her in a cat carrier. I feared this procedure would put back my attempts to gain her confidence.

I enlisted the help of a friend. Unexpectedly, it was not too difficult. She pushed back the bed and I cornered Tilly. She was still frozen immobile with terror so it was relatively easy to pick her up and put her into the carrier. She was literally stiff with fear in my arms.

She remained in a frozen immobile state on the vet's table and stayed silent in the cat carrier on the journey home. After her ordeal, I opened the carrier in the spare room and she shot straight into her hiding place. The invisible cat had returned under the bed.

'This has set things back,' I noted in the diary I was now keeping to chart her progress – or lack of it. 'Have I taken on too much?' I added.

A cat that was unable to come out in daylight was never going to find a home as a pet. If I could help Tilly live in the same house as humans, albeit with a minimum of human contact, she *might* eventually find a home. But how long was it going to take me to change her behaviour? Months? Years? I knew of people who had tamed adult feral cats but it had taken three or four years. Did I have the patience?

Nothing much changed for the next few days. Tilly ate and used the litter tray only at night. But as she was using the tray regularly, I decided I could at least start the process of changing the type of litter. The sort used by Cats Protection is wood chip pellet and these were flying round the spare room, thanks to her vigorous digging.

It may seem odd to start the business of changing her litter so early in what was clearly going to be a difficult relationship with Tilly, but litter-tray arrangements are a source of difficulty between humans and cats. Both get upset if the setup doesn't work out. Humans like to buy the type of litter they can best afford and site the tray where it suits them, often in the utlity room. Most cat owners clean it once a day.

Cats often have completely different ideas. They get used to the feel of a particular type of litter under their feet, and may refuse to use any other kind. They want their tray in a secluded place (far away from the roar of the washing machine) and they like it cleaned twice a day. Just to make the point, they will often watch their humans cleaning up the litter, then step in immediately to use the now clean tray.

My own preference is for fine-grained clumping litter, which allows me to scoop out the used sections easily. Tilly, however, was used to wood chip pellets. Could I persuade her that fine-grained was better?

I proceeded with caution. Each day, when I cleaned out the used pellets, I replaced them with clean wood chips plus a single handful of fine-grained clumping litter. The tray still had the familiar smell of damp wood, but each day the proportion of pellets to grains decreased.

'The signs are good,' I wrote in my Tilly diary, 'but it's going to take a long, long time.' After ten days or so, the proportion of pellets to grains was 50:50.

Then I changed the litter tray itself. I had originally put two in 'her' room. One was the smallish litter tray that I had taken from the Cats Protection pen. With such a nervous cat, it seemed safer to take the tray she was used to. The other was a much larger tray, of the kind I had used for my previous cats. At first Tilly would use the smaller Cats Protection tray only. Then I started putting small amounts of soiled litter into the other, bigger tray and after a day or two she used that instead.

The final change (for my convenience) was to see if she would use a hooded litter tray. I prefer a hood because it lessens the amount of litter that is thrown out of the tray. Cats are raging individuals and some of them will refuse to use a tray with a hood. Others, equally irritatingly, will refuse to use an open tray. Tilly was used to an open tray in the Cats Protection pen. Would she settle for one with a hood?

It turned out she would. 'This is my first easy success!' I noted in the diary.

Tilly remained invisible when Ronnie came home from hospital. I had organized a bed downstairs for him because he couldn't manage the stairs. Now I had a sick husband downstairs and a mentally sick cat (an unfair description of a possibly feral cat) upstairs. Nevertheless, I thought Ronnie might like to see Tilly in the flesh. It was time to start giving her a little more freedom. I began by opening the spare-room door at night, when all the outside doors and windows in the house were safely shut.

This appeared to make no difference at first. Ronnie and I never saw her. In the first week, it seemed that she still didn't dare move out of her room. She ate the food and used the litter tray there.

'Now look what you have landed us with,' said Ronnie with dissatisfaction as he settled in back home. His idea of a cat is one that is beautiful, graceful and well behaved. William, the most beautiful cat in the world, had been his cat. Tilly was ugly and ill behaved – the exact opposite of William.

'She's like a vampire,' he went on. 'She only comes out at night. I'd better get myself a crucifix in case she goes for my throat.'

Ronnie had loved William but he hadn't yet got to the stage of loving all cats immediately. He has to be won over by the charm of each individual cat. Truly dedicated cat lovers will put up with simply horrible cats. Take Dennis the Menace, for instance, a ginger tom who had lived on the street, been rescued and found a home with a cat-loving couple. He bit them whenever they came in range of his teeth, and warded off all attempts at affection with his claws.

Dennis had obviously not been properly educated to live with humans during his kittenhood. He was frightened of being touched. When stroked, he bit. This tactic worked well for him. Any human hand that unwisely tried to touch him beat a sharp retreat after he had bitten it. Dennis learned that biting kept humans at a safe distance.

Surprisingly, his humans adored him, almost as much as the local vet's surgery loathed him. Veterinary staff got bitten each time he was taken in. His owners had named him Dennis the Menace out of some kind of misplaced pride in him and were happy to tell their friends about his appalling behaviour, which they did in a doting tone of voice. They had fallen in love with their feline abuser.

Naturally, Dennis the Menace never sat on their laps, or purred at them. He showed no sign of affection towards them, although he might condescend to come and sit in front of them when he wanted food. He attacked them without mercy when they had to pick him up to take him to the vet. Yet his humans loved him dearly. Judged in the light of codependence (unhealthy caring), these were Humans Who Loved Cats – or, at least, Dennis – Too Much.

Ronnie did not suffer from cat codependence. Just the reverse. His attitude towards Tilly the Invisible Cat was not tolerant. Not for the first time, I began to wonder if one or other of them would have to be rehomed. This time Ronnie was in poorer shape than the cat, so it might be Tilly who would have to go.

And yet … It would be hard to find an adopter who would feed and care for a small brown cat who rarely came out in daylight. We would need to find an exceptional person, someone who wouldn't mind if the cat kept a safe distance from all humans and lived under the bed when feeling upset. That sort of owner is rare.

'I won't keep her. I *will* find her a home,' I hastened to reassure Ronnie. 'Promise. Cross my heart. I won't have her here for ever.'

For once I was telling the truth. I did not plan to adopt her myself. My job was merely to rehabilitate her as much as possible and then to hand her on to the kind of cat lover who enjoyed taking on difficult cats.

'You come first,' I told him. 'I love you more than a cat. I won't rehome you.'

The first sign of movement occurred when Ronnie and I began to notice small changes overnight. Newspapers – as journalists we have several delivered daily – were torn and small shredded pieces were found in different rooms. Wastepaper bins were upturned. 'She will only come out of her room at night when all the lights are off,' I noted in the Tilly diary. For the first time we could see that somebody else was living in the house with us.

Ronnie still had not set eyes on her. Then something happened to show that this little cat was beginning to feel at home in her territory. I never looked under the bed to see if she was there any more, in case my doing so frightened her. One morning, however, curiosity got the better of me and I decided to check if she was still huddled against the wall. I lay down on my stomach, lifted the bedspread and, to my horror, saw no sign of a cat.

'She's escaped,' I yelled down to Ronnie, in a panic. 'She's got out somehow. I can't find her.'

'She can't have,' he said. 'We shut all the doors and windows at night. She never comes out during the day at all.'

The litter tray had been used so she must have been in the house the previous night. She must still be in the house. Somewhere.

I couldn't believe it. Where on earth had she gone? I began the business of trying to find a missing cat. I looked behind the living-room sofa; below the chest of drawers, where there wasn't enough room for a cat but a cat would still squeeze under; in the darkest area below the stairs; behind the washing machine in the utility room; underneath the sink, just in case she had pulled the cupboard door open.

I pulled out all the drawers in the chest of drawers in the bedroom. William had once been discovered sleeping in a drawer and I had nearly shut him inside. I looked on top of the wardrobe and on top of all the kitchen cupboards – some cats like to hide high up. I checked in the blind area under my desk. I lay on my side to see if she had squeezed herself under Ronnie's desk.

I thought about going outside and calling for her, but what was the point? She was terrified of me and would run away from me rather than towards me. However, I did look in the garden shed just in case she had managed to slink out of the front door some time and had hidden there. I also went to the nearby barn and looked around. There was no sign of her outside, thank goodness.

Then I remembered that the door to the other bedroom had originally been open that morning. I had absentmindedly closed it after finding Tilly missing. The second bedroom has two beds in it. I lay down and checked the far bed – no Tilly. But under the other bed, there was the familiar small brown furry figure.

Tilly was huddled away from me, head lowered in fear, fur standing up, eyes absolutely terrified. Again, she had pressed herself against a far wall, but she *had* hidden under the bed that was nearer the door, as if she might want to look out. This could be a sign that she wanted to check her territory for danger before emerging; or it could be a sign that she was getting more relaxed.

I moved food and water into her newly chosen room, and put a second litter tray in there, leaving the other one in the small spare room. Instinct told me that, since she was successfully using the litter tray in her original room, I should leave it where it was. Cats will sometimes stop using the tray if their humans move it to a new location. So I left the tray there, and just put a second tray in her new room. 'Better safe than sorry for a damp carpet,' I wrote. 'But I hope she goes back there tonight.'

She didn't. The next day I checked both trays. Tilly had used the tray in the original spare room and not the one in her new room. She had eaten and drunk, so she was happy to eat in her new room but not to use the litter tray in there.

So this apparently feral little cat had taken over and occupied two rooms in my house. Now I could no longer have a friend to stay, because I no longer had a free spare room. It also meant that both doors had to be open in the day time. Tilly had decided she needed both rooms, one to be used as a bedroom and dining room, one to be used as a bathroom!

She was small. She was ugly. She was still terrified and invisible. Yet already she was changing my household arrangements to suit herself. Like all cats, she had strong views of her own, and she expected her humans to adapt to her wishes. It was an awesome example of how cats, even small frightened ugly cats, can manipulate their owners.

Admittedly, I'd had a minor success in getting her to accept new litter and a new litter tray. But she had had the major success of taking over 25 per cent of my living space.

Chapter 5

First contact

A powerful and unpleasant feeling of being watched woke me at 3am. It was like a horror movie when eerie music plays. A Thing was peering at me. Eyes somewhere out there in the dark were looking my way. I could not see the invisible stalker but I knew she was there. Gazing at me.

I was on my own at nights, sleeping in the upstairs double bedroom. Ronnie was still sleeping downstairs in the dining room, while we waited for a stair lift to be installed. His earlier fall meant that using the stairs was no longer completely safe for him. 'Old age is a shipwreck,' he commented gloomily, quoting General de Gaulle.

For a man who had reported first-hand on every North African and Middle Eastern war from the 1950s to 1990s, this was a depressing situation. He faced it stoically without complaint or requests for sympathy. He was glad to be home, even if it was a home he had to share with yet another cat. And at least an invisible cat would not be winding herself round his injured leg and tripping him up.

Sleeping separately, when we had spent most of the past 40 years sleeping together, felt lonely for both of us. I felt uneasy. I have always been frightened in the dark. As a child, I was always grateful when the family cats or dogs chose to sleep on my bed. The purring of the cats and the sheer weight of the family Labradors, Dinah and Paddy, were immensely reassuring. They held back the dark for me.

Now the dark had eyes. I sleep on the left of our double bed, a foot or two away from the open door leading to the landing. It was from the landing that I was being watched. That first night I found it so difficult to get back to sleep, after the unseen eyes had woken me, that I had to put on the light and read for a while. The eyes belonged to Tilly, of course.

I should have felt delighted that she was now confident enough to creep up on me and gaze at my sleeping form, but somehow I didn't feel good about it at all. The silent feline watcher brought back some of my childhood night terrors. To be observed without seeing the observer made me feel fear, which I knew was ridiculous, but I felt it all the same.

What if she sprung on the bed and attacked me? The rational side of my mind knew she wouldn't do that, but the emotional part of my brain recognized that there was a predator out there in the dark. I began to feel oppressed by this silent presence. It was like having a ghost in the house – unseen but always there. 'It's very creepy to know that I am being silently overlooked,' I wrote in the

Tilly diary. I thought that perhaps I could catch her watching me but once I'd woken up, I suppose my movements made her retreat immediately. I started trying to lie still and open my eyes without making any other movement, but I never succeeded in seeing her. Maybe she saw my eyes open and retreated then, or perhaps she caught some infinitesimally small movement that told her I was waking up.

Then the noises started, in the dead of night when all the lights were out. The first night it happened, I heard a small animal rush downstairs at about 3am. During the following nights, there were occasional thumps in the early hours, as some living creature jumped off a bed or a chair. She was heard but not seen. The invisible cat was now audible.

It was surprising how much noise could be made by such a small animal. As she grew more confident, I heard her running up and down the stairs several times in the middle of the night. She wasn't just racing up them, as if to run back to her hiding place. I definitely heard her racing downwards as well. Our stairs creak so it was easy to hear the direction of the sounds. She made quite a racket. I also heard scrabbling noises on the carpet outside the bedroom and scratching noises on the cat scratching post downstairs in the living room. I listened to the rustle of newspapers as she jumped on them and tore bits off them.

Our house wasn't very tidy. I don't like housework, and a succession of cats had already left their scratch marks on the soft furnishings, despite the lavish use of double-sided carpet tape to deter them. The side of the double bed still had the marks where Ada would wake us up. Half asleep, but still witty, Ronnie would greet her early morning scratching by mimicking the speaking clock and intoning: 'At the first scratch it will be 7am.'

Telltale signs downstairs on the living-room carpet still showed where William would scratch before leaping on to the windowsill. He spent a lot of time on the large windowsill, a place that no other cat, except Boomer, has favoured. Nearby, the scratching post still had dangling string, where Boomer had torn off the pendant cat toy. Each small bit of feline damage held a treasured memory for me.

Now Tilly was making her marks in our home in her turn. As well as newspapers torn at the edges and overturned wastepaper baskets, paper would be pushed off my desk and pens found on the floor below it. I started to leave little balls of newspaper around the house to see if they would take her interest. More often than not, when I found them in the morning, they would be in a different area of the room. She had to be *playing*. Why else would she move them around? Why else would she rush both up *and* down the stairs? This frightened and probably feral cat was actually enjoying herself, albeit at a time when no humans were awake to see her or to frighten her.

Since she had expanded her territory downstairs, I decided to go along with her decision. Until now she had been fed in her chosen bedroom, which also contained a litter tray that she did not use. The other litter tray, which she did use, was still in the small spare room that she had decided to use only as a 'bathroom' so to speak. It was time to bring food and litter downstairs.

I started with food, putting it down for her in the kitchen in the evenings. Cats prefer not to have water close to their food, so I put her water bowl down on a tray in the hallway. 'All the food in the kitchen eaten tonight,' I reported in the Tilly diary.

Then I saw her for the first time in the house, rather than under a bed. I was lying in bed reading and just before switching off the light I felt the sensation of eyes watching me. I turned my head slightly and she was visible sitting in the doorway. She could see me from there and could easily retreat into her bedroom if she wished. It was, I suspect, her usual watching place.

I dared not move. I did not want to scare her. Her pupils were already dilated with anxiety. She had seen that I had seen her. After about two minutes, during which I hardly dared breathe or move, she retreated to her room. It was a small step forward in our relationship and, I hoped, a big step towards her finding some kind of life in human society.

The following night, Ronnie had a similar experience. He heard her movements in the house and became aware of a presence. 'I thought it might be mice,' he told me. We had put his bed near the French windows into the garden. Artfully designed to be wild, the garden is hedged around with berried native species. It has plenty of shrubs for birds, and a wildflower meadow with long grass for insects and mice.

That summer there was a lot of wildlife out there – blackbirds, robins, guarding their territory by singing against all intruders, hedge sparrows that mate promiscuously, a visiting thrush, slender little wood mice with large round ears, visiting roe deer, the occasional hare passing through and even a colony of rabbits that had dug a warren under the shrubs. A person looking out through the French windows saw flowers and grass. A cat looking through those same windows saw a hunting ground.

At first, Ronnie merely noticed the long curtains twitching. It was around dawn, sunlight was just coming through the window and blackbirds and robins were singing.

'I pulled the curtain aside, and there was this small brown creature looking out,' he told me the next day. 'At first she was so entranced by the birds that she paid no attention to me. Then she ran off.'

He went back to sleep. He was taking a lot of painkillers for a back injury, so it was not difficult for him to drift back into slumber. Some time later he woke again.

'My toes were just sticking out of the duvet and there was a peculiar feeling at the bottom of the bed. I was being scratched, or rather tickled softly, on my feet. I sat up gingerly and saw a small brown furry face with those George Bush eyes staring back at me. Then she went scuttering off,' he recalled. That was the very first time he had seen Tilly in the flesh. Before that, all he had seen was her photo on my camera. He wasn't very impressed.

'My first thought was "What an ugly creature",' he admitted later. 'Then a slight spark of pity, or affection, crossed my mind.' From then on, every night he felt – even though he could not see for sure – that she was making a tour of inspection, checking him out.

I felt a pang of jealousy when he told me about his encounter with Tilly. True, Tilly had started coming to watch me from her sitting place on the landing. But she had never come close enough to touch me. Now she was actually pawing Ronnie. 'What's so unfair is that he doesn't much care if she likes him or not,' I wrote in my diary. 'I want her to grow to love me. Why isn't she pawing *my* feet?'

There was a reason, of course. Ronnie's indifference had attracted her. Cats often like people who dislike them. In feline society it is impolite to go up to others, make eye contact and introduce yourself. Eye contact is particularly threatening. The correct way for a cat to meet another cat is to ignore it, turn away the eyes and generally pretend it's not there. Humans who ignore cats are behaving just as a feline should.

I had failed to follow good feline manners. I had disturbed her by trying to look at her while she cowered under the bed. I had intruded into her territory daily to change litter or bring new food. Worst of all, I had even scooped her up and taken her to the vet. Ronnie, with the help of his relative indifference, had committed none of these impolite acts.

It was, nevertheless, pretty humiliating to see him being so obviously preferred. 'After all I've done for her! She's put me in my place,' I wrote. Then I added, 'That's what I like about cats. In feline eyes, a human's place is in the wrong.'

Despite her disadvantages, Tilly was beginning to exert the power of the paw! Ronnie was also beginning to take an interest in her. She may have been a scruffy little frightened cat but it looked as if she had that innate feeling of superiority to humans, found in all cats. She, not I, was setting the agenda.

In the next stage of rehabilitating her according to *my* agenda, it was time to move the litter tray downstairs. Just moving it, without providing an alternative upstairs, would probably be a bad idea, I thought. Cats need to feel safe to eliminate. Tilly was still reliably using the tray in her original room, so I didn't want to withdraw it yet. She had never used the one in her chosen bedroom, where she still hid under the bed for most of the day. Clearly, this was the one to move.

I put it in the utility room, adding just a little soiled litter from the used tray to it. That way it would smell like a latrine to her and prompt her to use it. Two nights later she did. So now she was using both a tray upstairs in the small spare room and one downstairs. Eventually, I would move the upstairs one downstairs – I like to have two litter trays for one cat – but I didn't dare do that yet.

However, I took the opportunity to vacuum the small spare room very thoroughly. Up to this point, for the duration of the two months or so she had been with me, I had not cleaned either of her upstairs rooms. The more they smelled of her, the more she would feel safe. I didn't want to interfere with the scent until she was more secure. What is housekeeping compared with making a small frightened animal a little bit happier?

A week later there was trouble in the litter tray, or, rather, trouble *not* in the litter tray. Tilly stopped using either tray for solids. A day passed without a deposit. Then a second day. Up to this moment I had been so focused on her emotional state that I had forgotten to worry about her physical wellbeing. Conscientious cat owners pore over litter trays, like Roman augurs studying the entrails of chickens to foretell the future. We read the runes of the paw marks there. We ponder the deposits as if they are omens of what might happen next. As indeed they sometimes are.

I got the litter-tray message. There was a hair problem. Tilly was a long-haired cat, and her fur was soft and fluffy. The most obvious reason for her constipation was not some horrid cat disease, but her own hair. Cats swallow their hair while grooming and it can literally clog up their intestines. The hair can either cause constipation or be vomited up as hairballs. (Hairballs have the wonderful scientific name of trichobezoars. *Tricho* means hair and *bezoar* means a ball of swallowed foreign material.) You know you are a cat lover when you laugh as you get out of bed and put your bare foot on a hairball first thing. The other joy of life with cats is hearing your cat beginning to barf up a hairball as it lies on or in the bed with you. The barfing up usually takes a fair few throat-clearing noises before the trichobezoar appears.

Tilly was beginning to shed a lot of hair. She needed brushing. Not only had I not brushed her for about two months, but as things were, I saw no possibility of brushing her in the future. I could not get near her. Indeed, I was only permitted to see her at a distance.

For the time being laxatives were the answer. They speed up digestive transit and reduce hairballs. Nowadays, they come as cat treats. So all I had to do was add four or five laxative treats to her food bowl and litter-tray use started up again. I had solved the problem of her long hair affecting her digestion. What I hadn't realized was that other problems would arise from her lack of being brushed. They were to become evident later.

My plan to give this little cat the ability to live happily in a human house was proceeding very slowly. She now occasionally emerged from under the bed during the daytime. She would sneak downstairs when we had left the house to do the shopping, or when we were both busy at our computers, or perhaps while we watched TV in the evenings. She ate in the kitchen. I did not see her at the food bowl or in the litter tray but the food disappeared and the litter tray was used.

Next I began to catch the occasional daylight glimpse of her at the top of the stairs. This was the landing from which she had started watching me at night. From this position she could see me in the hall, or at my computer in my upstairs office. More importantly, the landing was the ideal place from which she could speedily retreat. And each time I caught sight of her, that's what she did. She whisked back into her room and straight under her preferred bed. She was still not ready to take part in our family life.

Her body language on these occasions showed how scared she still was. At each encounter she would be sitting up, poised for flight. If I ignored her or stayed absolutely motionless, she might stay for a few seconds. Then her ears would go back, her tail down and she would scamper away. If she saw that I was gazing at her, she didn't linger at all. A direct look was enough to prompt instant flight.

More than two months had passed and she was still only semi-visible, spending a lot of time under the bed, even if she was using the rest of the house at night and sometimes during the day. 'Rehab is proceeding very sluggishly,' my diary read. 'Is it going to work?'

The plan was to get her used to the sounds of TV and CDs being played, dishwasher and washing-machine noises, the ring of the doorbell, the sound of vacuuming and the clatter of plates and cutlery being laid on the table. As far as I knew, Tilly had not been exposed to the activities of an ordinary household. In the cat pen where she had lived for 18 months, awaiting adoption, there were none of these things. She was an innocent.

In theory, by now she should have been becoming more relaxed around humans, or at least less frightened of Ronnie and me. The shock of the new usually diminishes over time. If she could grow accustomed to me and my presence, perhaps she would stop being terrified of sharing space with other human beings. Then she might be fit for life as a pet and somebody could adopt her.

Trying to induce cats or people, whether children or adults, to be less fearful in this way doesn't always work. Sometimes, the process of just getting used to something goes into reverse in a development known as 'sensitization'. The cat becomes *more* sensitive to what it fears, rather than less. The fear may even start spreading to other areas or become a general phobia. The same is true of humans.

In a 1920s experiment that I consider unethical, scientists paid the mother of a nine-month-old baby, Albert, to see how he developed fear. He was introduced to a white laboratory rat and played with it with confidence. Then the scientists made a frightening noise, by banging a steel bar with a hammer, each time the rat was put near him. Poor little Albert was terrified by the noise, and he became very scared by the rat, too. He learned that the appearance of the rat meant a frightening noise would follow. Soon his fears started spreading and he became scared not just of the white rat, but of a white rabbit they showed him, and then frightened of anything furry at all.

Was this happening to Tilly? Were her fears growing rather than diminishing? When she was in the Cats Protection pen, she had just begun to let Ann very occasionally stroke her gently down her back. Nothing like this was happening with Ronnie or me.

I had expected her to take a few weeks to settle and get used to living in a house with people. It seemed to be taking months. If she was truly a feral cat, taming her would involve several more months, even a year or two. 'I feel I am getting nowhere,' I wrote.

The only encouraging sign was that she hadn't made a run for it, escaping out into the garden. I had kept the cat flap locked throughout her stay but the back door was occasionally open during the day, as we came and went. If she had been determined not to live in a house, she could have escaped much as Boomer had done. She didn't seem determined to do that.

'I must face the fact that she may not ever make a suitable pet,' I wrote in despair in the Tilly diary. I got a friend to install a cat flap in my garden shed. If Tilly was going to be an untameable feral cat after all, I might have to keep her outside, away from the household noises that frightened her so much. The garden shed would at least be weatherproof and I could probably install some heating in it if I needed to.

This was not what I wanted but it might be what I would have to settle for. As a cat tamer, I appeared to be wholly incompetent.

If I so much as glanced at her, she responded with terror. The only close encounter had been when she had patted Ronnie's feet. I was on the edge of giving up.

Then it happened – the moment when I realized that she was not a completely wild or feral cat. The moment that changed everything.

Once again, I was in bed reading before putting out the light to go to sleep. She was sitting on the landing looking at me, while I tried not to look at her. I just glanced sideways out of the corner of my eye, hoping she would not notice. She was about 2 metres or so (8 ft) away from me, a little less than her normal minimum 3 metres (10 ft) safe distance from which she could run away.

Suddenly, she rolled over on to her side. She was performing what cat scientists call 'the social roll'. It's a come-and-play signal, often given by pet cats towards their humans. An invitation for attention, and may be even an invitation for a stroke. The ears are forward, the eyes are friendly and the cat is exposing its tummy.

She was doing it. And her eyes showed she was doing it towards me. Very carefully and slowly I put down my book and made little kissy-kissy noises towards her. I didn't get up or move towards her. I didn't dare risk spoiling the moment.

She rolled a bit more, still looking at me, then got up and walked slowly back to her room.

Chapter 6

The cat who saved my life

When Tilly rolled on her side for the first time while looking at me, it brought back memories. It wasn't just what she did. All my much-loved cats have performed the social roll towards me. It was the unexpectedness of the roll and the weirdness of it happening when she was still apparently so fearful. Her sudden moment of friendship reminded me of Ada, the black-and-white cat who was responsible for turning me into the complete cat lover.

Ada, the cat whom I had adopted after she had given birth to a kitten in my garden shed, showed a similar extraordinary mixture of fear and confidence, from which I pieced together clues about her early life. On the one hand, she would run away and hide outside if there were raised voices or sudden movements in the small Regency house in London, where we then lived. She felt safer outside than inside.

An extreme example of this occurred in 1987 when a small hurricane swept over London. Ada insisted on being let out at 5am at the height of the storm. Any other cat would have cowered indoors in that howling gale. Instead, she went to the back door mewing so insistently that she woke me up. Too sleepy to realize what was happening outside, I let her out right into the hurricane. I was distraught when I woke up later and discovered that a quarter of the trees in London had fallen in this high wind. I had let her out into danger. Luckily, she survived and came back inside during the morning.

She had lived on the London streets for so long that when she was scared, she was desperate to get outside, and be back in her old territory. She felt safer in urban spaces than indoors. At this point in our life in London, we had a terraced house with a small back garden. On one occasion, when something in the house had scared her, she climbed out of a second-floor window. Honeysuckle grew up the house and she scrambled down that to the ground. When a visitor arrived at our weekend country cottage in Somerset, she would often jump out of a top window if she found one open.

We didn't have a cat flap in London, and she would signal her desire to go outside by flinging herself against the back door to see if it would open of its own accord. Later, when she had learned that she needed me to open it, she would fling herself against it repeatedly because it made a banging noise that attracted my attention.

Although she displayed a loving attitude towards me, my presence did not make her feel safe. Tilly's restricted life in a cat pen made her hide under a bed when she was scared. Ada, whose early adult life had been spent outside on the streets of Westminster not far from the Houses of Parliament, would insist on getting out of the house when something frightened her. If we had friends staying, she would come in for her meals and go straight out again.

At the end of our garden was a building with a flat roof, leading to the back of a high block of flats. At times when she felt stressed, Ada sat on this roof refusing to come down. At times of terror, she disappeared altogether.

Oddly enough, she never, ever, tried to leave by the front door of the house, which opened into a small street leading to some playing fields. That particular street, with its window boxes and railings, was not her path. The walls and roofs between flats and our row of terraced houses at the back were her pathways. Cat routes differ from human routes.

Living inside the house all the time with her kitten had obviously been difficult for her, and when Billy had gone to his new home, she spent a lot of time outside, whatever the weather. She continued to raid the cat food from other houses in the street and was once caught sleeping on my next-door neighbour's sofa.

I fear she also terrorized one or two of the neighbouring cats. She was a big cat and would attack anybody in 'her' territory. Once when I tried to intervene with bare hands in a cat fight, she bit me very hard indeed. When an inch of feline canine teeth penetrates your thumb, it is excruciatingly painful!

Usually she came back dry from her excursions, so I assumed that somewhere along the back of the houses she had found a refuge. Somebody else's garden shed perhaps? Under a car? Underneath a building? In one of the old coal bunkers under the pavement? Circular covers allowed Victorian coal merchants to pour the coal straight down, and the bunkers were accessed through a door in the house's basement – plenty of scope for a resourceful cat. Like many other cat owners I had no idea of her mysterious other life, what she did or where she went when she was not in my sight. Feral and stray cats need a dry place to sleep, if they are to survive. It is as important as food to an animal whose ancestors originally came from the dry desert rather than a wet climate. She must have had a dry hideway somewhere.

Ada wasn't truly feral, however. She craved human touch. While she was responsible for her kitten, she kept her distance from Ronnie and me. Then, after the kitten had left, she suddenly flopped down in a social roll for me.

'What are you doing, Ada?' I said to her. 'Do you want your tummy tickled?'

She did. Just as I suddenly saw Tilly lying on her back looking at me, so Ada all at once switched her attitude to me. She was still frightened, nervous and anxious almost all of the time but increasingly she would flop down in the social roll. Unlike most cats, she adored having her tummy stroked. Many cats roll over winsomely and then grab your hands with their claws if you try to touch the exposed tummy. Ada never scratched or bit when I did this. I could bury my face into the soft fur of her tummy, and she would purr with pleasure.

This affectionate behaviour alternated with her insistence, at moments of stress, in staying outside altogether. But even in the early days when she was clearly anxious all the time in the house, she never bit or scratched – except for that one occasion when I interrupted the cat fight. During her kittenhood, she must have learned to be gentle with humans and to retract her claws during any human contact.

Nonetheless, she took months to settle down to domestic life. For a start, she couldn't believe her luck in getting regular meals. She never assumed that the next meal would turn up. Instead, she ate everything she could get her paws on. No food left out in our small basement kitchen was safe. She would bite through a plastic bag to get at a packet of biscuits and then eat a quarter of them. She would push lids off pans and lick dirty dishes. She tore open egg cartons with her teeth and bit right into the eggs. She would eat one or two eggs completely, licking out the white and the yoke and crunching up some of the shell. The remaining eggs she would bite open but leave half eaten.

In her first year with me she would routinely pull down all wastebins in search of food. She would sort through the rubbish for anything edible. She knew how to tackle the now old-fashioned dustbins, too. She would stand on her two back legs, pull down the bin with her paws and examine the contents in the hope of finding an old bit of chicken skin or fish head.

Her taste in food reflected the upmarket nature of Westminster, her home territory. She was intensely fond of paté, garlic sausage and ham, delicacies she had presumably sampled during her days of scrounging food while living on the street. She was a high-status scavenger. They say that cats regulate their food intake so that they don't get fat. She never did. Naturally, a cat who was eating stolen biscuits, raw eggs, dustbin scraps and a tin of cat food a day risked putting on weight. Within six months, sleek black-and-white Ada had become a rather portly figure.

Despite her growing bulk, she could curl and squeeze herself into the small furry cat bed that I bought for her when she was still slim. Every single night she slept in it on the landing, just outside my bedroom. I still have the old and battered bed. None of the other cats who lived with me wanted to use it. Perhaps they sensed that it still belonged to her ghost. Then Tilly, in some kind of sisterhood with Ada, started using it and still does so today. As a small cat, she fits in more easily than Ada did.

Ada grew fat. Not quite obese but definitely fat. 'She has a certain *embonpoint*,' remarked the late Sophie Hamilton-Moore, daughter of a major general, who ran the Stonehenge Cats Hotel, my boarding cattery of choice at the time. 'She's well found,' was her other thoughtful and delicate comment on Ada. Miss Hamilton-Moore (I never dared use her first name) was another legendary figure in the world of cats. In the 1970s she ran a cattery information service, producing a list of catteries that she considered to be up to her high standards.

Miss Hamilton-Moore, a self-styled 'dedicated eccentric', inspected scores of these establishments but just five met her exacting requirements and went on her recommended list. Her own Stonehenge Cats Hotel headed it up with five stars. I was terrified by her and used to make my husband telephone any time I needed to alter a booking. Ada, on the other hand, took an immediate and unexpected fancy to her. Ada was therefore regularly boarded there when we went on holidays.

Ada's preference for me over Ronnie, and for Miss Hamilton-Moore over any human other than me, suggested that she had not been introduced to many men in her kittenhood. Men worried her. She took such an intense dislike to Ronnie's brother that when he came to stay with us, she spent all day outside, coming in during the early hours to eat her food. Something about him upset her badly. I wondered if it was the clerical collar he wore (he was a vicar). Was Ada a committed atheist like Professor Dawkins? Did she object to Christianity, a religion that sadly has no place for cats in its Bible? More likely the reason lay in his attempts over the years to win her confidence. Even when she had consented to stay indoors when he was there, she would disappear upstairs if he so much as looked towards her. The slightest move of his body in her direction or an attempted call of 'Puss' had the same effect.

Her distrust of Ronnie took months and months to disappear. I don't think she realized that he had threatened to leave me because of her. Nevertheless, until the very end of her life she was wary of him if he came home having had a drink at Fleet Street's famous bar El Vino's. Perhaps in her kittenhood home she had suffered at the hands of a drunken man. Or perhaps, in her life on the street, drunks had shouted at her or thrown things at her.

Ronnie's equal distrust of her also took months to disappear. He did not really want any kind of pet but as a peace-loving person he also didn't want a running battle with me. 'The secret of our successful marriage is that I always do what she tells me,' he often jokes to others. I think the secret of our successful marriage is that both of us try not to interfere with the other's life too much.

Just as I accepted his frequent absences from home while visiting war zones, he put up with Ada's presence in the home. I knew he had finally accepted her when I came home to find him serenading her with *Abide with me*, the hymn sung in classic style by Victorian contralto Clara Butt. 'She likes *Abide with me*,' he maintained. And certainly she looked as if she might.

Ada was a difficult pet, alternating between affectionate flops on the floor and complete disappearance. She particularly hated transport by car, a necessity in her life because at this time we spent each weekend at our country cottage. Somehow she knew when we were planning to leave and would disappear into the back garden to sit on the flat roof, out of reach. There she would stay, mewing plaintively at five-minute intervals, as if taunting me. Even if I managed to shut all doors and windows beforehand to keep her inside the house, she could still disappear. I would spend hours searching the back of the sink, underneath each bed, in the black hole area behind my writing desk, in the broom cupboard, in the clothes cupboards, in left-open drawers, on windowsills behind curtains. For a portly cat she could squeeze into unbelievably small gaps and unexpected places.

She was particularly clever at hiding in places that were apparently in full view. Thus she would sit on the seat of a chair that was pushed in under the table in the dining room. She would hide behind a half-open door or squeeze herself behind the sofa. And while I was in full hunt, she would silently change her hiding place as I moved on into another room. Meanwhile, Ronnie would be fretting at our delayed departure. 'Can't you get that bloody cat in? Why don't you just leave her. We will get caught in the rush hour.'

Naturally, any movement of mine towards the cat carrier set off this game of hide and seek. But I used to wonder how she knew what I planned *before* I touched the cat carrier. Did she recognize the words 'vet' or 'cottage'? It seemed unlikely.

More likely was that she had noticed some tiny action on my part that gave the game away. Before taking her to the vet, I would take out her vaccination certificate, and she may have recognized this move as a forerunner to putting her in the cat carrier. Before going to the cottage, perhaps she noticed me packing food or clothing.

I grew more and more careful, trying to leave packing to the last moment after I had her safely stowed in the cat carrier. But she still knew. Some people think cats have extra sensory perception. I don't. I think they draw conclusions from the tiny moves of their human owners. Perhaps she followed a clue such as the direction of my eyes towards the cat carrier, as I planned a journey.

Even worse were her disappearances when we were planning to return from the country to London. Ada's super-sensitive radar would detect what we had in mind. Her method then, as in London, was to refuse to come in. Even at the cottage, she still felt safer outside than in. She would sit in the garden in the fading light doing her intermittent mewing. Her persistence was legendary. In turn, we would pretend that we were not leaving at all.

Hours would go by. We would unpack the supper we had planned to eat in London and eat it in Somerset. We would turn on the TV, partly to drown the reproachful mew from the garden, partly to trick her into believing we were settling down for another 24 hours. On one or two occasions, we even undressed and went to bed, staying alert for her arrival through the downstairs open window. This then required a cautious walk down the stairs, trying to look casual, and a quick slam of the window. A half-hour hunt later, she would be in the bag. At 3am we would be driving back up the A303, exhausted but in time for work the following day.

At first, the country baffled her. She had led her life among the back gardens and streets of Westminster, where foraging for food meant overturning dustbins or breaking into other cats' houses to eat their food. She had never hunted live prey, not even the pigeons that are common in London. She had never caught, and never did catch, a rat. Catching rats is a skill some cats never pursue – rats bite hard if a cat does not time its kill-bite with deadly accuracy.

Ada's first six months weekending in the country were spent cautiously investigating grass instead of paving stones, and fields instead of flats. While the farmyard cat next door, Jouffy, brought a constant stream of dead mice and rats to the farmhouse door, Ada caught nothing at all. The dustbins of the small Somerset hamlet where we stayed must have been a disappointment, too. Nobody there ate the garlic sausage or paté that she preferred.

Even when she did begin to hunt mice, she seemed not to know how to go about it. I remember seeing her deposit a mouse on the lawn, bat it with her paw, and then yelp and retreat when it bit her. She sauntered off with a look of feline indifference, which made it clear she had lost all interest in the mouse and something quite other had caught her attention. It took her six months to learn how to hunt, and a further six months before she would eat any of her prey.

Once started, however, the innate drive to hunt that exists in all cats kicked in. She learned how and when to pounce, and how to kill her prey. Soon she became an enthusiastic hunter, spending hours in the Somerset countryside in pursuit of mice. From being a cat that could survive as a stray on the London streets, she became a cat who might have survived as a farm cat.

She was a living example of why cats are one of the most successful animals on our planet. Cats live in the backstreets of huge cities, in African slums, the Australian bush, Greek dockyards and on islands uninhabited by humans. They are masters of survival and have spread throughout the world, hitching a lift on ships but capable of living without further help. They adapt themselves superbly to local conditions and may well survive when our species is extinct.

Ada's growing mousing ability had one unfortunate side effect. Not only did she regularly bring in the little corpses, but she enjoyed hiding them in unexpected places instead of leaving them where they could easily be seen. She hid them under bathroom mats, pushed them under armchairs, behind sofas, inside the open doors of wardrobes, or dropped them under radiators where the heat speeded up their decay. She once placed a dead mouse in my open handbag and, on another occasion, carefully inserted one into a paper file where I was collecting receipts for my income-tax returns.

I suppose I should be grateful that she never went so far as my friend's cat, Gismo. He hid a dead mouse in the toaster overnight. My friend came down for breakfast, placed a single slice of bread in one side of the toaster and out wafted the smell of toasting mouse.

As Ada became a better hunter, she started bringing in living mice. People who don't have cats think that getting a cat will mean fewer mice in the house. Overall this is probably true – the mouse population will drop in a cat's territory. Nevertheless, the cat may start bringing mice into the home to eat later or just to provide a bit of fun at 3am. Ada dropped one into the storage drawer below our double bed. We didn't notice it at first. It was only after a fortnight of sleeping above strange scuffling noises that we discovered it was there. In the meantime it had shredded my father's hand-made lace christening robe, utterly destroying what was a masterpiece of lace making, in order to make its nest.

'We never had mice in the house till we got a cat,' complained Ronnie. 'Damn that cat.' He still found some aspects of living with cats tiresome. While he was beginning to see the grace and charm of the species, he was not yet fully tuned into living with felines.

Cats who have not been handled in kittenhood are said to be 'unsocialized' to humans. My husband was 'unsocialized' to cats – he hadn't been exposed to cats when he was young. Slowly, however, he grew first to like Ada, and then to love her. Just as she had to learn that living indoors was safe, he had to learn that she was a delight, not just a burden. The friendship between them took time to develop.

I became more and more bonded to her. In the morning she would uncurl her stout body out of her small cat bed and do a series of stretches, just about the time I slowly opened my eyes.

She never slept on the bed with me, but she enjoyed getting on my lap. As she was large, she overflowed it and I had to keep her steady with my hands to stop her toppling off.

All her life she remained unpredictable. She would flop on her back exposing her belly to me several times a day, hitting the carpet with an audible thump, accepting strokes, tickles and even kisses. She would sit on my lap with pleasure, giving an imitation of a true lap cat. Then, a sudden movement on my part or an unexpected noise would make her hurtle to the back door to be let out. In a second or two she would turn from lap cat to wild cat, staying out of the house for several hours. She alternated between intense friendship and intense fear.

She needed me as her gateway to a domestic life. At first I didn't realize how important that was going to be for me. When she had been with us for about five years, I began very slowly to go downhill into a pit of depression. I did not realize what was happening because in outward ways my life was unaffected. My freelance journalism seemed to be going well and Ronnie and I were happy together.

Depression is a strange experience because it happens within rather than without. There was nothing wrong in my life, no incident that set off this growing feeling of unworthiness and fear that my friends disliked, even despised, me. I stopped all activities that gave me pleasure – visits to the opera, listening to baroque music, going out to eat. I avoided mirrors because what looked back at me was so ugly. I could not bear to look at photographs of myself.

Focusing on others became the way to avoid these feelings. I collected emotionally needy people who would ring me at all hours of the day, asking for my sympathy. One woman would call up to four times a day. Several times a week I visited an old lady who was a compulsive talker. I spent hours listening to waves of her unceasing speech. She was passive, sitting in her little flat complaining that nobody came to see her. I would sit there listening to the long involved sentences and the huge irrelevancies of her inner monologue, which would range backwards and forwards over 50 years of her life, a life with very little incident and much unhappiness. In any half an hour, she would speak for 25 minutes or more. I might be given five minutes to speak. She had forgotten, if she ever knew, the rules of give and take in conversation.

If I was tired, I did not rest. If I was unhappy, I did not cheer myself up by doing something nice for myself. If occasionally I gave myself a break, I felt guilty. I had to be good and do good. As well as compulsively helping others, I worked very hard at my job. Just as I could not turn down a request for help, I could not turn down work when it was offered to me. As a self-employed worker, I had a lousy employer.

I gave money to others rather than spending it on myself. I stopped buying clothes. My underwear was grey and tattered.

I simply could not buy new knickers. Sometimes Ronnie would have to buy clothes for me, because I did not feel I could spend the money on myself. I bought kitchen equipment from charity shops, even though I could have afforded to buy it new. Spending rather than giving away money became increasingly difficult. I did too much almost every single day. I was exhausted every single night. And still I felt I was not doing enough, that I myself was not enough.

Self-sacrifice became important to me, not for some good reason, but because it meant suppressing my loathed self. If Ronnie wanted to do something I didn't want to do, I would do it, not just because he wanted it, but because it was my duty to suppress my own wants and needs.

And through all this slow descent into hell I didn't notice what was happening.

I'm not sure when the first thoughts of suicide began. But increasingly suicide felt like the next thing on my agenda. It would relieve this world of my obnoxious presence in it. Self-destruction felt like a duty. I began working out how to do it so as not to inconvenience anybody else. And while I was pondering whether to throw myself under a bus (unkind to bus drivers) or overdose (tricky because there was no Google then to tell me how to do it), the idea grew more and more compelling.

Occasionally, I would sit in the corner of the room rocking backwards and forwards like an animal trapped in a cage. The repetitive movements were somehow comforting – although not comforting enough.

One morning I woke up with the fully formed idea that I should kill myself that week. I ought to do it. I didn't deserve to live. Nothing in the world was wrong except my presence in it. It was me, my very self, that was disgusting. I should make this world a better place by taking myself out of it for good.

I looked at Ronnie as he got up to go downstairs for breakfast that day and thought, 'He will be much happier without me. I am blighting his life.'

I thought of all the people in my life that I cared about – my elderly father and mother, my sister, my brother, my friends – and concluded, 'They will be better off without me, too.'

Then I looked at fat Ada, who had just completed her morning stretching routine and was about to go downstairs for *her* breakfast. The thought that saved my life then came to me. 'Ada needs me. What will happen to her if I kill myself. She just won't be able to manage to live with Ronnie. Even if he could look after a cat, he'd never manage to care for her properly. She is just too difficult.'

My mind at its sickest still knew that she really needed me. An ordinary uncomplicated pet cat would have been able to live and bond with Ronnie or been adoptable by someone else. Ada with her nervous reactions would have been difficult to re-home. And at that time, in the 1980s, when up to a third of cats handed into mixed animals shelters were put to sleep, she would have been on death row.

So my death would have probably meant her death. Her need for me gave me something to live for. It says something for the disturbed balance of my mind that I didn't think how horrible it would have been for Ronnie if I committed suicide. The illusion that he would be better off without me held strong sway. I wasn't able to believe how upset my mother, my father, my sister and my brother would have been. But I knew Ada might lose her life if I killed myself.

Thanks to that thought, a glimmer of good sense came into my mind. 'I am ill,' I thought. 'I need help.' I found a therapist that day, began going once a week, and slowly fought my way out of the depression that nearly killed me. Friends and acquaintances of mine have not been so lucky. They have died from this potentially fatal illness. They didn't have a fat, difficult cat to help them cling on to life.

Ada had saved me.

Chapter 7

Tilly's courage to change

Tilly seemed to adapt to family life even more slowly than Ada had done. That single moment, when she had rolled in front of me, did not recur for several days. However, I now had a glimmer of hope. I no longer believed that she was just a feral cat who would, at best, be a wild creature that I had tamed. It seemed to me that she was at least partly domesticated to human life. She was perhaps only semi-feral.

I might be able to help her to become a proper pet. Not a cuddle cat, of course, but a cat who would interact with humans in a reasonably positive way. Plenty of cat owners have cats who avoid being cuddled, refuse to sit on a lap and dislike being picked up. That independent spirit is what some of us enjoy in cats. We will often put up with feline bad behaviour and not even try to change it, although cats can be trained. This was going to be the next stage in my rehabilitation of Tilly.

Food is usually the key to making cats love you. Cupboard love, as it's jeeringly called, is a good way of training an animal to do what you want. There's nothing wrong with cupboard love.

It is like fair pay for an employee. Most of us go to work for a salary. Appreciation and thanks influence us too, but the salary is the real thing.

Cats are like us. They work best for reward, which for them is usually food, not just a few strokes. Yet there's an extraordinary belief among ordinary people that animals should work 'for love of us'. I have heard dog owners, who themselves unashamedly work for money, object, 'I don't believe in bribing my dog to do something. Praise should be enough.'

Would they like to work for nothing? Or get a pat on the head instead of a proper wage packet? I think not. They ask a level of devotion and selflessness from their dog that they would never ask of themselves.

Punishment is the other way of making animals and people do what you want. Some people wildly overestimate what animals can learn by punishment. Did my father really think that torturing my cat Moppet by putting a paraffin-soaked corpse round his neck would stop him hunting birds? Did he believe that Moppet would understand what it was about? That the paraffin corpse was somehow connected with the kill he had made several hours earlier? This was far too difficult a thought for a mere cat, I believe. Or did my father merely feel the satisfaction of knowing that Moppet had paid a price in suffering for what he had done? I shall never know.

Many people opt for punishment. Some find it easier or

cheaper to punish rather than to reward people or animals. Others unthinkingly punish animals and children because they are told it is the right thing to do. Punishment is still the traditional way to train animals and children. You can watch sickening TV dog-training programmes in which 'trainers' strangle dogs with leads, kick them, shout at them, 'show them who is pack leader'.

Yet neither humans nor animals give of their best for punishment. It's an ineffective training tool. Animals are usually too frightened to learn well from cruel masters. Fear makes it difficult for them to concentrate, so they learn more slowly. That means they need more punishment. It's a vicious circle. Reward, on the other hand, gives them the joy of learning.

Some cat owners still punish cats. If the cats do not use the litter tray, the owner will rub their noses in the mess. This is a totally ineffective technique. Cats punished in this way often take to house soiling even more, out of fear.

Reward is another matter. Like most animal behaviourists, I knew that I could influence Tilly's behaviour by making it worth her while to do what I wanted. 'What gets rewarded gets repeated' is the trainer's motto. Just as people repeatedly turn up for work in order to receive pay, so animals repeat behaviour in return for food. The idea was that I would lure Tilly nearer by giving her treats.

She was getting two pouches of cat food each day, put down in her food bowl morning and evening. For this she did not need to do anything at all. This was food she got 'for free'. She did not even need to be present and mostly she was not. She would be sitting at a distance, or still hiding under the bed. She would creep out to eat the food either at night or when I was not in the room.

I did not withdraw this food. Under stress in a new home she needed the security of knowing she would be fed whatever happened. Regular meals at regular times are good for both cats and humans. A sensible routine diminishes stress and makes for a feeling of wellbeing in both of us. I wanted Tilly to feel secure, not just for her own welfare, but because she would learn better.

She may have been a small cat but these two pouches were not quite enough. She could live on that amount but she wouldn't feel completely satiated. Up to this point, I had been giving her some extra dry food in her bowl. Now the extra dry food would come directly from me. First, I would throw it a distance away from me and eventually I would hand feed it to her. It was to be her reward for coming closer. These treats were simply good, balanced dried cat biscuits, better for her health than too many junk cat treats.

I put dried cat food in jars all over the house so that I had access to it quickly. When I saw her standing at her safe distance away from me (usually about 3.5 metres/12 ft at this stage) I would grab the jar, get out some cat biscuits and throw a couple towards her. The idea was to reward her for coming closer and let her associate me with the pleasure of the food. It didn't work. The mere movement of my arms was so frightening that she would immediately run away. By the time the cat biscuits landed on the floor, she had gone. Sometimes, she had disappeared before they had left my hand.

'She's so frightened of my throwing gesture, I wonder if people have thrown stones at her,' I wrote in the Tilly diary. 'Maybe the neighbours? It's no fun living near a property where 20 or 30 cats use your garden as a latrine. I will have to stop throwing the food.'

I decided to have cat biscuits ready in my pockets, then lie down on the floor and *roll* them towards her. Getting down to her level should make me less threatening and rolling rather than throwing ought to prevent her taking fright at my waving arms.

That didn't work either. I was 66 years old and getting down to floor level took time. By the time I was flat on the carpet she had run off. Even if she was still visible at a distance, she ignored the cat biscuits. Only if I got up and walked away, would she sometimes go back and eat them. Usually, I had to be out of her sight before she dared do this.

I tried taking off my glasses, in case these made her feel I was staring at her – staring is intimidating to cats. That made no difference either, except to make it more tricky for me to get down to ground level. By now, several pairs of my trousers had stains on them, because I had put them through the washing machine forgetting to remove the cat biscuits. Cat biscuits merge together in a sticky mess when washed. They do not dissolve!

Most ordinarily frightened cats would have responded to

food rolling. Not Tilly. She had been so traumatized by humans that she had learned to avoid them before anything, good or bad, could happen. Every time I moved anywhere near her, she felt fear. She wasn't going to wait around long enough to find out that I wasn't frightening.

Scientists call this avoidance learning. They tested it (cruelly) on dogs in a so-called shuttle box, partitioned into two areas by a low barrier. A buzzer went and an electric current on one side of the box gave the dog a shock. The dog discovered it could avoid the pain of the shock if it jumped over the barrier to the other side. So now each time the buzzer went, the dog jumped and avoided the shock before it happened.

The scientists then wanted to know how long it would take the dog to learn that the 'shock' side of the box was no longer dangerous. They stopped giving the electric shock, but the dog didn't stop jumping. Each time the buzzer went, it jumped. It wasn't going to risk even the possibility of an electric shock. It never stayed long enough to learn that the shock didn't occur. When you think of this, it makes sense. No sensible animal, or human, waits around for the infliction of pain if there is an easy way to avoid it before it might happen.

Tilly was like that laboratory dog. She had learned that human beings were threatening but that she could avoid them by running away. So she wasn't sticking around long enough to learn any different. She just wasn't going to risk it. And a few cat biscuits weren't going to change her mind. Fear is such a powerful emotion that it shuts down appetite. If you offer an ice cream to a soldier in the middle of hand-to-hand fighting, he wouldn't stop to accept it. You don't feel hungry during a car crash. Bodily systems, including digestion, close down. In their place a rush of emergency adrenaline powers the human or cat for flight or fight. This is what was stopping Tilly taking any notice of the food.

When she ran, she felt a rush of relief and the fear stopped. This feeling of relief from fear was influencing her far more than the hope of food. In every way, the relief was a far better reward to her than cat biscuits.

We now know why. In both animal and human brains a particular area just above the eye sockets is activated when the animal or human is rewarded. This expectation-reward-decision area is called the orbitofrontal cortex. When scientists delved further into this in humans (thankfully not animals this time), they found that this same area is also activated when the human avoids something unpleasant. The brain, it seems, treats relief from fear as if it was a reward. Well, safety is a reward, after all. So by avoiding me, Tilly got this rush of relief, not unlike the feeling of pleasure when given food. Running away felt good to her.

That meant she would continue to avoid me in order to get that feeling of relief from fear. So what was I to do? I couldn't force her to stay still, so that she could discover I was not a threat. I couldn't even get the cat biscuits to her in time before she fled.

Yet somehow I had to find a way to reward her for not running away. It was a puzzle and a challenge.

I dreamed up an alternative. I would be the one to run away.

'If I run away, she won't have to,' I told Ronnie that evening. 'She won't have to avoid me because I am already avoiding her. She can get the reward of feeling safe while holding her ground.'

'I suppose it might work,' he replied.

'It's the principle of negative reinforcement. It's training theory,' I lectured him with growing enthusiasm. 'It's rewarding Tilly for staying still instead of running away by the withdrawal of a negative stimulus, which is me. This method is just as powerful as positive reinforcement, using food rewards. My running away should really work. And it's not cruel, like some negative reinforcement might be.'

At this point I could see Ronnie's eyes beginning to glaze over with boredom. 'Very interesting,' he said politely, as he checked his iPhone. 'Very interesting' in that tone of voice means 'very boring indeed'. Sometimes I pity him having to live with me! Training theory, with its fourfold possibilities of positive reinforcement, negative reinforcement, positive punishment and negative punishment, *is* very boring to outsiders. Even after years of learning it, I still find it difficult to remember.

Ronnie hadn't taken much notice when his mad 66-year-old wife was getting down on her stomach to roll cat treats. He refuses to be embarrassed by my behaviour. Yet the first time he saw me running away from Tilly his reaction was not what I expected.

'Thank God for that. You're getting fed up with that cat at last,' he said.

'I'm training her,' I retorted. 'This is rehab.'

'Funny kind of rehab,' he grumbled.

I didn't bother to explain negative reinforcement again. He didn't need to know. I just continued stumbling up or down stairs, leaving the living room or even leaving the house altogether by the back door to get away from a small brown cat.

I wasn't actually *running* fast. It was more like actively avoiding her at a fast walking pace. All the ground-floor rooms are connected in our house, so it's possible to get to any room by two different routes. Every time I saw her blocking one way, I would immediately retrace my steps and go the other way.

Occasionally, I *had* to walk past her, particularly if she was upstairs where the house layout is different. The bedrooms all lead off an L-shaped landing. When I had to pass her on this landing, I was careful to avoid all eye contact. Cats are tuned in to human eyes. They are good at following the human gaze. They can see if you are looking at the cat carrier with the vet in mind, and thus make a run for it. They use gaze to communicate.

Staring, however, frightens them. So, in order to avoid intimidating Tilly when I had to pass her, I would fix my eyes upon something well above her height. I would walk past at the greatest distance possible and I would try to move my whole upper body round so my back, rather than my front, was facing in her direction. On these occasions she would still move away from me, but not at full running pace.

It began to work. The little brown cat in my house no longer ran away quite so far or so fast. If I had to pass nearby her, she would move back but not automatically run right back into the bedroom and right under the bed. Her eyes were still huge with fear and she was still spending about half of the day under her bed, but I was seeing her out and about in the house more and more. She was now able to sit and watch me at what she felt was a safe distance. And this safe distance was getting smaller every week.

Mostly these wary encounters took place on the landing. I would see her near her room and her chosen safe place under the bed, but she would now sit less than 2 metres (6 ft) away from me. Her 'flight distance', the distance she needed to keep between us before she made a run for it, had almost halved. I don't think I realized quite how significant that was at the time, but in retrospect it seems a huge achievement for both of us. She no longer needed a distance of 3 metres (10 ft) or more to feel safe; less than 2 metres (6 ft) gave her enough reassurance.

So it was time to go back to the original technique of using food to get closer to her. If I met her any closer than her preferred distance, I still turned on my heel and retreated. But if she was sitting still at that safe distance, I would lower my body, lie on my stomach and roll cat biscuits towards her. She was now so much more confident that these arm movements no longer terrified her. She would watch me with caution but no longer felt impelled to run.

I was always hopeless at ball games at school, and I'm even worse now, so my aim was poor. Sometimes the biscuits would not reach her, and she would wait a bit, then cautiously get up and go towards them. Often she didn't go right up to them but paused and then used her paw to hook the biscuit nearer. It helped her keep her distance and she must have felt safer that way.

But fear was no longer shutting down her appetite. She felt relaxed enough to eat in my presence. Really terrified cats can't do that. And she also felt she could take a few tentative steps towards me. Finally, she was beginning to think of me as a good source of tasty food.

Making the mental link between me and food is what we call associative learning. Cats do it and humans do it. Think of dating. If a man takes you out on a date for a delicious meal and makes you laugh throughout the evening, you begin to associate him with good food and enjoyment. Repeated experiences like this make you anticipate a good time when you see him. He is linked in your mind with pleasure. This can become the beginning of a loving relationship.

Tilly and I began the loving side of our relationship with food, too. We dated, so to speak, with cat biscuits, the feline equivalent of a candlelit dinner. She was still getting her basic rations of two pouches of food daily, so this was a fun extra, not an essential. I didn't want to blackmail her into loving me by keeping her really short of food.

Our relationship started to grow. She was now fairly confident that I was not going to move towards her and attack her, although she still whisked away if I came too close. She also became accustomed to the idea that I would lie down and roll dried food towards her. The flight distance between us halved again, so that she became comfortable with only a metre (3 ft) between us.

I began calling her name when I lay down so that she would begin to link her name with the offer of food. I don't think cats recognize that their name is a symbolic representation of themselves. To them it's just a sound. But I do think they recognize that particular sound, and understand it as some kind of call signal, a way to get their attention, and even a way to ask for their presence. If it becomes a signal that food will be offered, they will often (if not always) come when called. It may take a bit of time for them to arrive, particularly if they are doing something interesting in the garden. A cat will ignore all human calls while mousing. In most circumstances, however, calling the name and giving food works. I was teaching Tilly to come when called, like you teach a dog!

One day when I was in the living room, she came in and stared at the TV (she is interested in activity on the screen). I lumbered down to floor level and she came and ate the food that I rolled about a metre (3 ft) away. Then she moved off a further half a metre (2 ft) or so, and rolled on her back.

The second social roll had happened! I was jubilant but I stayed still, careful not to respond with any sudden movements. She looked at me in an inviting way, got up and left the room. The rehab programme was working, and we continued to make progress.

'She is sort of coming when called now,' I wrote in the diary. 'She will take food from my hand if I am lying down.' Next I no longer had to lie on the floor. She would take food when I was sitting in a chair if I lowered my hand to her level. Her ability to be around me without fear was increasing daily.

Her body language changed, too. She no longer slunk round the house with her stomach close to the floor, tail drooping. The tail wasn't bolt upright yet in the sign of a happy cat greeting a friend, but it had raised itself to half mast.

One day I found her sleeping *on*, rather than under, her bed. She jumped off and dived underneath as I approached but it was good to know that she was now sometimes able to sleep on the bed, even leaving a few cat hairs to prove it. She probably slept on the bed all night when I was not moving round the house.

Then the wonderful moment happened.

I was sitting on the sofa watching TV, not thinking about her. I was on the left-hand side, so there was plenty of room for a cat to sit on the other side. Not all my cats have been willing to share the sofa with me. William the Beautiful, her predecessor, usually preferred to sit at my feet or on the windowsill, a cool place for a cat with a lot of hair. Only near the end of his life did he sit near me on the sofa.

His predecessor Little Mog had always shared the sofa with me. She never came too close, preferring to maintain a discreet distance, but she would look at me affectionately, and purr.

Neither of those cats had been a cuddle cat, nor had I insisted that they become so. I was just humbly happy to accept whatever degree of closeness they allowed me. I knew both of them loved me but I also knew that both of them liked their own space. I respected that. They decided for themselves how much intimacy they would allow me. I acquiesced in their decision, even when I wanted more.

I was not expecting Tilly ever to become a sofa cat.

I was absorbed in the TV programme when she suddenly jumped up beside me. Without even thinking – and if I had thought, I would not have done this – I put out a hand to stroke her along the back. Suddenly she rolled on her back, collapsing with her legs apart. She was so close that her body was nearly touching me. Her little brown-grey tummy was exposed to me. Tentatively, I stroked her gently on the chest between her forelegs. I didn't dare stroke lower for the time being. She wriggled with pleasure and spread her legs even further. I started stroking a little lower, the soft fur of her tummy, the sensitive part of it.

Neither William nor Little Mog would have allowed me to do this. William would have gently bitten me. Little Mog would have got up and left. Tilly merely wriggled some more and started purring loudly. She was craving for my affection.

It was a revelation of both her past and her future. She had found the courage to change her behaviour. The terrified feral or semi-feral cat had suddenly morphed into a relaxed domestic cat.

She was a pet, a real pet, after all.

Chapter 8

Fur and purrs

What is it about the soft touch of fur? I don't mean the cold fur of dead animals, bred and confined in cages, slaughtered, skinned and made into a coat for a rich woman. Even my father, who was quite capable of cruelty to animals, despised those people who wore fur just for the luxury of it.

His own mother, my grandmother, was usually swathed in fur. She would visit us in winter, chauffeured cross country from Kent in her pre-war Rolls-Royce, wearing a huge mink coat down to her ankles. The coat had to be long because she had never given up the Edwardian skirts of her youth despite living into the 1950s. The coat, for which many minks had suffered and died, was almost as wide as it was long in order to accommodate her bulky figure. In spring and autumn, when the dead mink coat was back in the cupboard, she contented herself with two dead foxes hung round her neck. The teeth of one fox in a rictus grin clasped the furry tail of the other. Their glass eyes glared in the terror of their death. Only in high summer was her outfit free of dead animals.

The soft warm fur on a living animal is so different. Some people, myself included, have a craving for the sensation of a warm furry body. Maybe this is left over from our monkey and ape inheritance. Do we need to stroke a furry body, just as a baby monkey needs to clasp his mother's fur? For a monkey, the need for touch is so overwhelmingly important that he will prefer a furry substitute mother that gives no milk to a wire substitute mother that does give milk.

For me, no touch of human skin has ever been so comforting as the fur of a living dog or cat. Of course, when it comes to sex, it is the touch of the naked human body that I enjoy. But for affection and comfort and security, the soft fur of a living creature is what I long for. I have wanted the touch of furry animals from the time of my early childhood. I refused dolls altogether in favour of teddies and soft toys. Later in childhood, I used to push my face into the warm flank of the friendly family dogs or, if they would permit it, against the warm neck of my father's large hunters as they leant out of their loose boxes.

Few of my cats have ever let me do this to them. Surprisingly, Ada, the first cat of my adult life, did permit me to bury my face in her soft warm furry tummy. She craved my touch as much as I craved hers. It is not just touch. There is the delicious smell of clean healthy animals, too. That is part of the enjoyment of contact with them. Each species has its own agreeable smell. I didn't expect Tilly to let me put my face close to her body. It was enough that she had a craving for human touch. I was just grateful that I could stroke her at all. I was charmed by the way she would collapse on her back and ask for affection.

Never during her 18 months in the cat pen had she been so friendly. Ann had been able to stroke her back occasionally but that had been all the contact she had permitted. So the little brown cat's sudden invitation to me to tickle her tummy was an extraordinary switchover, a magic transformation from terror to love.

I was delighted, of course, but tickling her tummy revealed a problem. The soft fur of her belly was knotted into little solid mats of hair. There were mats under her forelegs in what would be the armpits if she were human. There were little mats under her tail and down her thighs, mats on her chest, and what looked like bigger mats in the ruff of fur round her head.

Mats matter. Once they have formed, it becomes more and more difficult for the cat to get rid of them. Worse still, they seem to attract more hair so they grow bigger and bigger. As they grow, they pull tighter and tighter and finally begin to pull on the skin below. Sores develop under the mats. The skin itself can be torn.

Tilly's extensive mats were very bad news indeed. I had to conclude that she was not grooming herself. There had simply been no room for her to do so under the bed, where she had spent the best part of two months. However, this couldn't be the whole explanation, because she was now spending time above the bed and in the rest of the house.

Then I realized I had never ever seen her grooming. This should take up quite a big proportion of a cat's waking day. It is an instinctive behaviour, wired into their brains. They probably spend eight per cent of their waking time grooming themselves, using their teeth, nibbling and pulling at their fur. That may not sound a lot but it's about the same amount of time that indoor cats spend eating and drinking. Tilly wasn't keeping herself and her fur in good condition.

A cat with mats is an unhappy cat. Very elderly cats sometimes cannot twist round to groom themselves properly. Hugely fat cats, like Big Boomer, may be unable to reach various parts of their bodies. Cats that have an underlying disease may stop grooming. These are common reasons for lack of grooming. None of them applied to Tilly.

Was she just a natural scruff? I did not think so. It seemed more likely that she had emotional reasons for not grooming. She may just have been too frightened to settle down for a good wash. After all, a cat cannot be on full alert for enemies while grooming. She might not have dared to groom at all because she was almost always scared and anxious.

Perhaps another reason was misery. Really miserable cats, like really miserable people, lose the energy to look after themselves. There have been times in my life when I felt I was not worth looking after, and times when I was so busy caring for others that I had no energy to care for myself. I had spent a year looking after my mother before she died of cancer, so focused on her care that I forgot, for weeks at a time, that I needed care, too. I stopped having my hair done, wore no make-up whatsoever and was too exhausted to shop. I had, however, unlike Tilly, always washed myself!

During that year, my unstyled hair and thrown-on clothes had been the equivalent of Tilly's mats. Poor little cat. I realized that I had underestimated her despair. After all, three-quarters of her life had been spent in the Cats Protection pen and, while she was obviously not happy there, she had adapted to it. Familiarity is comforting. The change of being suddenly placed in a new home, in a house not a pen, had put her under enormous stress.

Grooming is also a way in which some animals develop bonds of affection. Being groomed may stimulate the brain to release the affection hormone, oxytocin. There wasn't much affection in Tilly's life in the pen. She did not love, but merely tolerated, her companion cat, Lottie. She must have further despaired of affection when she was dumped in a strange house with unfamiliar humans, Ronnie and me.

Not being able to groom while she hid under the bed would have made her feel worse; or maybe the hair had got so tangled that it hurt her to try to groom out the mats. What was unusual about her behaviour was that she didn't use grooming to help her deal with stress. Cats often do a bit of quick grooming after they have had some kind of worrying encounter. But if the stress is too chronic, maybe some cannot manage grooming at all.

I phoned her previous fosterer, Ann, to ask, 'Did she develop mats when she was living with Lottie in the pen?'

'No,' said Ann. 'She didn't have any.'

'Did you see her washing? I've never seen her washing herself.'

'Sometimes I did.'

I felt a pang of guilt. In the short term, far from helping Tilly by taking her into my home, I had actually made her worse. I had to do something. I was going to have to help her get rid of the mats and then I was going to have to groom her regularly. I have always brushed my cats, even those with very short hair, and they have always enjoyed it, so the latter task was not going to be a big deal.

But there is a downside. If you tug away at a cat's hair and hurt him, he will learn that brushing hurts and may refuse to be groomed. Some pedigree cats, including Persians, Maine Coons and Norwegian Forest Cats, come into rescue shelters ready to bite anybody who brushes them. Yet they have such thick fur that they *need* daily brushing. If I tackled Tilly's mats by myself, we might end up in the same dilemma.

Tilly's coat was not as thick as a Persian's, but was longer than a shorthaired cat's, about 8 cm (3 in) in length. The fur was very soft and fluffy, like a pedigree Birman's coat – had her mother met a Birman on the fields of her native smallholding? – with no strong, thick guard hairs, just a few black ones on her tail.

At this point, even her tail had a few small mats near the base. If she had been as friendly as Boomer, it would have been easy. I would have done the same as I'd done for him – merely asked a cat-friendly person to hold her while I cut off the mats with blunt scissors. Once Boomer had lost enough weight, he had been able to reach round and keep his own backside free of them. I know cutting off mats with scissor leaves the fur looking irregular, but who cares!

It wouldn't work with Tilly. She was totally phobic about being picked up and held. I felt that the attempt might end in my hurting her if she wriggled. Some of the mats on her tummy were very close to her soft tummy skin and armpits, and it would be easy for scissors to slip on a struggling cat. Besides, there were far more and far bigger mats on her coat than on Boomer's. If I hurt her, she might never trust me again.

Veterinary help was the only safe solution. I don't trust dog groomers to groom cats. At a veterinary clinic they could give her a mild sedative before cutting off all the mats. They could also examine the skin underneath to make sure there were no sores, and if there were, treat them. Most important of all, if she was traumatized by the experience in the surgery, there would be no fall-out for our relationship. She would blame the vet, not me. I could start daily, or near daily, cautious brushing with a clean mat-free feline – or so I thought.

I had previously taken her to the vet without great difficulty. It had been in the first month of her stay with me and I had cornered her, with the help of a friend, by simply pushing the bed out and picking up the terrified cat underneath. It had been easy because she had been frozen with fear.

This time was different. By now she was using the whole house and, while she would retreat under the bed if stressed, she was equally likely to be found in any of the other rooms. If I had been sensible, I would have left an extra half hour just to get her in the cat carrier. Better still, I should have called a friend to come and help me with her. I did neither.

Luckily, I did make some preparations, although not enough. I closed off all the bedrooms upstairs – cornering a cat by moving the bed is only possible if there are two of you, one to move the bed, the other to pick up the cat before it moves *with* the bed. Cats are not stupid. They are quite capable of simply relocating themselves so fast that they remain in the middle of the moving bed area, safely out of anyone's reach.

I closed various downstairs rooms where there were too many hiding places. Thinking I would be clever, I decided to corner her in the kitchen, using food as a lure. She liked her grub and would come and eat if I was careful not to reveal what I had in mind. I placed the open cat carrier on the kitchen table and pushed a pillow up against the gas stove, so that she would not be able to squeeze herself underneath it. I locked the cat flap.

Preparations completed, I rattled the food container, in she came and I closed the kitchen door behind her. Like a competent general planning a military operation, I reckoned my tactics would be successful. But cats have a way of outwitting humans. I bent down to pick her up from the floor where she had her head in the dish. She shot away to the other side of the kitchen. I went after her, thankful that I had remembered to block off the space under the gas stove. In the past, living mice had been brought in and stashed there by William. My attempts to rescue them had taught me it was impossible to drag any living animal out of that dark space. Poking out a mouse corpse had been difficult enough.

By the time I got to the other side of the kitchen she had run away again, with a surprising turn of speed for so small an animal. Then I lost it. If I'd had my wits about me, I would have stopped the pursuit, made a cup of tea and pretended to lose interest. Lulled by my indifference, and tempted by more food, she might have settled down to eat again. I might have been able to make a more successful second attempt.

But I hadn't left enough time and I was panicking that we would be late for the vet. (As if vets aren't used to cat owners ringing up to say 'I can't find Tibbles'.) So I continued the pursuit. She dashed across the kitchen, on and off the table, on and off the cookery books on the windowsill, all of which fell down and scattered on the floor. She jumped in and out of the sink, behind the coffee maker, and even on to the kitchen stove itself.

Finally, I cornered her near the door and made a grab. That was my biggest mistake. I hung on tightly while she twisted and turned and nearly wriggled free. My hands clasped her lower body. I had no purchase over her head.

She was terrified. Turning towards me, she clawed at my face, breaking the skin from the top of my left-hand forehead, down over my eye, across my cheek to my chin. Only the fact that I wear glasses saved me from a serious scratch to the eyeball. One finger was also badly scratched.

I managed with great difficulty to shove her ruthlessly into the carrier that was standing open on the kitchen table. She braced her front legs to try to refuse to go in. By now she was behaving like a wild cat, and a completely distraught cat has the strength of ten. She was almost impossible to handle. I forced her in somehow, and jammed the door shut just before she could whip round and escape.

There was blood dripping down my face and my finger. I was panting and heated from the chase. 'A vicious cat' is what an ignorant onlooker might have said. 'Vicious' is the unfair word we apply to animals that hurt us. Yet I knew she wasn't vicious. She had just been completely traumatized. I mopped up the blood with the kitchen towel and washed the scratches with antiseptic. Cat scratches can be harmful. On at least one occasion I have had my whole hand swell up, thanks to the bugs on cat's claws. It's always worth taking scratches seriously.

I hadn't got time to worry about, or even think about, what had happened. I put the cat carrier in the car and drove to the veterinary surgery. 'Be very careful with Tilly,' I warned the nurse. 'She's a frightened cat and may need cautious handling.'

'Did she do that?' she asked, pointing at my face.

'Yes,' I replied. 'But it was my fault. I didn't handle her right. She's very frightened, which is why I can't deal with the knots in her hair on my own. You may have trouble getting her back into her carrier. She hates being picked up.'

I left Tilly in the vet's surgery and drove home in deep depression. 'This is a huge setback,' I wrote in the Tilly diary when I was back at my word processor. 'I don't know how long it will take to get back to a friendly relationship. A long time, I think.'

It had been my fault. *All* my fault. This was a good example of ignorant, although not deliberate, human cruelty. I knew very well that the first rule with terrified cats is that you must make a plan on how to handle them – not just chase and grab. Yet I had chased and grabbed and the result had been a shocked little cat and a big scratch down my face.

Only by the grace of an animal-loving God (yes, I believe in a God that loves all animals including human animals) had I escaped serious injury to my eye. Worse still, I had put Tilly's whole future at risk. After this, she might never trust me again. She had already spent 18 months waiting for a proper home and never finding someone willing to love her.

Things had been going so well. I had had hopes that I might be able to rehabilitate her so that she would become a loving, ordinary pet cat. The whole episode had been not just a mistake, but a seriously stupid mistake.

I rang the vet's surgery later in the day to ask how it had gone. 'The knots are off and she's coming to after the sedative,' they told me.

'Do be careful when you put her in the carrier,' I warned them again. 'She struggles very hard indeed.'

When I arrived at the surgery, I warned them for a third time.

'Oh there's no trouble with that,' the nurse said. 'She's already in it. We put it in the pen with her and she's gone inside of her own accord.'

I felt guilty and ashamed as I drove home with her in the back of the car. Cats, unlike dogs, are not forgiving animals. They never forget a traumatic encounter or a real enemy. They never forget an injury, either. Cats, unlike dogs, have no methods for making up after a fight.

I put the carrier in the hall and opened it, having shut all the outside doors. I feared that the trauma of our last encounter might lead her just to pack up and leave home. My only comfort with this gloomy thought was that the garden shed had a cat flap, so if she decided to leave the house, she would at least be able to shelter there.

I expected Tilly to rush up the stairs and huddle under the bed again. 'More knots,' I thought. 'The invisible cat will be back. I may have to start running away from her again!'

She walked out, shook herself, looked up at me and went straight to the food bowl. I had placed the evening pouch of food ready for her. She ate it. That was promising. Less promising was that afterwards she went straight upstairs to her room. But she walked rather than ran upstairs.

I had decided to ignore her and get on with my ordinary activities, avoiding eye contact and pretending she was not there while she was eating. She and I both needed time to recover, to reflect and to see if we could be friends again. I hoped that we could but I thought it might set the relationship back by weeks if not months.

That evening as I sat on the sofa watching TV, to my surprise she came into the living room. She sat and looked at me for a bit, as if trying to make up her mind. Then she jumped up next to me, rolled on her back and let her tummy be tickled. She had forgiven me.

Cats don't forgive and forget. I know that. Yet, against everything I knew about feline behaviour, Tilly had just done so. Wiser than I am, she had picked up our relationship at the point where it was before being so rudely interrupted by my impatient behaviour and her terror.

After that, preventing the knots appearing again in her fur was so easy that I could not believe I had been so worried. I already had a soft brush. I just started brushing her with this each time she got on the sofa beside me. She loved it. I loved it. I found a tiny remaining knot that the vet had missed about a week later and cut it off easily with a pair of scissors. She didn't flinch or even move.

Then I started using a comb as well as a brush. She was happy with that, too. I could not believe my luck. She need never have a knot again, because I could comb right through almost all of her hair – even the little hairy breeches at the back end. I had never had a cat so happy to be brushed at the backside. She was the perfect long-haired feline pet.

Nevertheless, I could not ignore – as she had so generously ignored – what had happened. As a fosterer, I had let her down and she, as a result, had injured me on the face. It took three weeks for the scars to disappear and I was lucky the scratches did not get infected. During those three weeks, I had time to reflect not just on my own stupidity, but on her reactions. True, she was a pet cat, but some trauma in her past meant that she could never be a completely safe pet.

Cats Protection couldn't let her be adopted into a home with a baby or very young children. Under stress, she might scratch deeply again. This loving little creature by my side might hurt a baby or a toddler – not out of viciousness but out of a re-awakened terror.

There was also another reason why re-homing her was going to be difficult. Me. My feelings. They say that the falling out of friends is the renewing of love. As Tilly lay on her back beside me that evening, I thought, 'She really needs me. She loves me.' And then I thought, 'I really love her.'

Reader, I adopted her. She was no longer a Cats Protection foster cat. She became *my* cat and I became *her* human.

Chapter 9

Chips, catteries and carriers

We were eating fish and chips for lunch at the table in our kitchen – Ronnie loves fish and chips, associating them with happy memories of his childhood – when Tilly, with unexpected boldness, jumped up on to the table. This was the first time she had dared jump up while we were sitting there. She grabbed a big chip right off my plate, leaped off the table on to the floor and gobbled it down in one go, swallowing it almost whole. The chip vanished in about 30 seconds.

I have never seen a cat eat a whole chip before. And I have never seen a cat eat something that fast. My previous cats had occasionally nibbled at a chip, but they had never fancied scoffing a whole one.

'Even Ada never did that,' was Ronnie's reaction. I noticed a tone not of condemnation but of admiration in his voice. His attitude towards her was becoming warmer. She had not exerted the full power of feline charm on him yet, but he has always enjoyed the sheer cheek of cats. I had to stop him throwing her another chip on the floor! Chips cannot be good for cats.

The speed and intensity of her theft was so eccentric that I decided it was time to play cat detective. I must pay more attention to her daily behaviour, in the hope that it would give me an insight into her early life. A sound, a smell, a context can trigger relapse into early feelings in both cats and humans. Just as my father had marked me for life, the experiences of her kittenhood had marked her. If I was to help her become more normal, I must become her therapist and delve into her past by looking at her present odd patterns of behaviour.

Stealing the chip was not an isolated instance. Now that she was getting more confident, her thieving increased. One afternoon I went into the kitchen and found a half-eaten plain boiled potato on the floor. Another potato was missing from the pan I had unwisely left on the worktop. There had been four potatoes and now there were two and half. She had eaten one-and-a-half boiled potatoes. I could hardly believe that a well-fed cat would eat them in the first place. There was no butter on them to make them palatable.

On another occasion I left a surplus of mashed potatoes in the saucepan, forgetting to put it away in the fridge when it had cooled. About a third of the mash was missing. She had eaten it. Cats are meant to be completely carnivorous but I seemed to own a cat who was hooked on carbs.

'Today in the morning I found she had eaten a large chunk out of half a slice of wholemeal bread,' I wrote in the Tilly diary.

'Yesterday evening I put down a ham sandwich ready for Ronnie and I found her almost choking on it. She seemed as eager to eat the bread as the ham. Ada would have pulled out the ham and left the bread.'

Oddest of all was her raid on an unopened packet of crumpets. English crumpets are spongy things tasting of nothing at all until they are toasted and covered with loads of butter. She had eaten three-quarters of an untoasted, unbuttered crumpet.

Her thefts grew more frequent and more eccentric. That first winter she would go out into the garden and eat the scraps of bread I had put out for the wild birds. She would roam round the kitchen flagstones like a vacuum cleaner in search of crumbs. She stole digestive biscuits, cake and once some uncooked pastry. She was beginning to show signs of saggy tummy syndrome.

'Ronnie has started making a klaxon noise and yelling "cat alert" when he sees her near any food,' I wrote in the diary. Clearly, Ronnie was no longer just tolerating her. Now he found her amusing. I overheard him saying to her, 'How now, brown cat?' Talking to her was a good sign. Soon he would love her, I hoped.

I know just one other cat with somewhat similar food tastes and that's Herbie, my nephew Jess's 7 kg (15½ lb) heavyweight British Blue. Herbie has chav eating preferences. He won't eat freshly cooked chicken or turkey but he will eat cheap reconstituted chicken roll, chicken nuggets or turkey twizzlers. He likes corned beef out of tins but refuses fresh steak. He relishes spam but turns up his nose at fresh ham. Jess, who has had Herbie from kittenhood, thinks he knows why.

'Herbie came from the back garden of a breeder who lived in social housing,' he explained. 'He has the food tastes of the woman who bred him. I fear she wasn't very well off and she fed him from her own table.'

Tilly's preferred diet was even worse than Herbie's. She was not interested in any kind of meat, whether home-cooked or otherwise. She didn't bother to steal eggs or fish. She did, however, do dairy. Milk can be bad for cats, so I never give cats milk. Tilly stole milk whenever she could, polishing off the remains of Ronnie's daily porridge if she could get it.

Once I cooked a tiny fillet steak for Ronnie when he was ill with a bout of chronic obstructive pulmonary disease. I was hoping to tempt him to eat. He left most of it and, as I don't like fillet steak, I cut it up and offered it to Tilly. It was raw in the middle and cooked on the outside. She would not touch it.

You can take the kitten out of the slum but you can't take the slum out of the cat, runs the pessimistic old saying adapted to felines. Eating preferences are learned early in life. Chips, potatoes, bread and milk were, I deduced, what Tilly had eaten on her native smallholding before she was rescued. Herbie might have been fed from his breeder's table. It looked as if Tilly had been fed from the supermarket reject bin. No wonder she was so small and ill in her early life. A carbohydrate diet must be bad for a carnivore.

To find out more about her early upbringing, I rang Olivia of Cats Protection, who had originally helped rescue Tilly.

'I was told that some of the cats found with Tilly were kept in an open-sided barn,' Olivia explained. 'There were tea-chests on their side full of straw as beds. We didn't organize the rescue. That was the RSPCA,' she went on. 'We just took some of the cats. There were scores of them, both inside and outside the house. Lottie and Tottie [Tilly's original name] were both quite ill when they came in. They were not litter trained, either, so we think they may have come from the barn.'

Here was a possible explanation for potatoes, plain bread and milk. It looked as if the owner of the smallholding had fed his cats the cheapest food possible. Many people who end up with a collection of 20 or more cats cannot afford to feed them properly, or get them neutered, or pay for proper veterinary care. Welfare experts call these people 'cat hoarders'. They don't mean to be cruel but the cats' welfare suffers.

Tilly's odd food thefts were a pointer to this kind of upbringing. Despite having been well fed on proper cat food by Cats Protection for the next 18 months of her life, she had kept her kitten food preferences. It was the feline equivalent of yearning for your mother's Yorkshire pudding.

I made one attempt to put a complete stop to her food thefts.

I thought that perhaps if I gave her as much cat food as she could eat, she would stop stealing. On the first day I left a huge bowl of dried cat food for her, so that she could eat all she liked throughout the day. She did. She ate the whole bowl – the equivalent of three days' food. I filled it up the following day. She emptied it again. A third day I filled it up. She emptied it again.

Then I lost my nerve. I did not dare go on with the experiment. Cats are meant to regulate their food intake. Tilly did nothing of the kind. By the end of the three days she had a tummy as tight as a drum and was too bloated to do anything much but sleep. And during those three days she had nevertheless found time and motivation to steal yet another slice of dry bread.

It wasn't going to work. So I decided that in the future I would just have to be more vigilant about putting away all carbohydrate and dairy foods. I hadn't cured the problem but I could manage it.

The next insight into her early life came when I put her in a cattery for a week. I was not very happy about doing this, but it was my first chance of a holiday for three years. Ronnie, who had been intermittently ill for all of that time and longer, was currently having a good spell.

For years he had lived with neuropathic pain, after a helicopter crash when he was reporting on a conflict in Oman. Old age had added to this a catalogue of conditions that was impressively long. His resolute acceptance, first of chronic back pain, then of multiple life-threatening diseases, was admirable. Indeed, he was always optimistic and sometimes almost frivolous. When told he had peripheral vascular disease, which means the blood doesn't reach the extremities, he merely commented, 'Well, if it's only peripheral, it can't be too bad.'

He reckoned he would like to visit his native Yorkshire, God's own county, as he considers it, quite wrongly, of course. Everybody knows that Somerset is God's own county! I didn't care where we went. I was just longing for a week in a hotel with somebody else doing the cooking.

I felt bad about putting Tilly in a boarding cattery but I knew that she would be safer there than in my home fed by a stranger. My next-door neighbours, who would have been happy to feed her, are only in residence at weekends. Tilly had spent about four-fifths of her life in a Cats Protection pen, so she would be accustomed to cattery conditions. She knew the score. Besides, I desperately needed a break.

I chose the best local cattery I knew, run by a woman I trusted, but I still felt unhappy about it as I delivered a fearful Tilly, crouched in the carrier, into the pen. When I opened the carrier, Tilly bolted right into the closed area of the pen and refused to come out. I had taken some of her bedding, so that she would at least have the familiar smell of home, and went in to arrange it in the cat bed. Tilly was cowering in the covered litter tray. I warned Joan, the cattery owner, 'Tilly is very shy. You may not see much of her.'

I was not expecting Tilly to enjoy her stay. Several of my cats have stayed at this well-run cattery and, while none of them have particularly enjoyed it, they have come home in good condition. They have survived the experience.

Some cats are less resilient. Herbie, my nephew's British Blue, is so upset in a cat pen that Jess brings his own foam cat house. This is placed inside the covered area of the pen and Herbie sits in it all day, only coming out at night. Since Herbie is so big, there is not much room in his foam house, but he has to be fed inside it.

I just hoped Tilly would not be so terrified. I left her with a heavy heart, feeling that I had consigned her to prison. Parents who take their children to boarding school probably feel something similar.

'How did she do?' I asked Joan a week later, when I came to collect her.

'She wouldn't let me touch her but she did come out into the run when there wasn't anybody around,' she replied, as she led me to the pens. 'She didn't mind the cats next door to her, either.'

I was expecting Tilly to welcome my arrival, but not a bit of it. She showed no sign that she recognized me, let alone liked me. When I came to pick her up, she shrank away from me, hissing as if she had never met me before. Her body language was extremely hostile. Her ears were back and she looked as if she might bite or scratch. Fortunately, she merely huddled immobile in her bed, stiff with fear. This allowed me to pick her up and put her in the carrier, which I had brought with me.

The laid-back ears and the hissing suggested that I was no longer her friend. Had she really failed to recognize me? Surely she wasn't that stupid. Was she punishing me for leaving her in the cattery in the first place? Surely she wasn't that clever!

My guess was that re-awakened fear had made her revert to feral behaviour towards me. She may even have been experiencing something a little like human post-traumatic stress disorder. Her memory of 18 months in a cat pen had come back in full force. Perhaps the cattery stay had reminded her of those sad days when she was the ugliest cat in the shelter, when people came to visit her, took one look and rejected her.

If so, the memory disappeared altogether back home. 'When she walked out of the carrier, she behaved as if she had never gone away,' I wrote in the Tilly diary. 'She spent her evening next to me on the sofa as always. It turns out she hasn't developed any mats in her hair. So she has been keeping herself nicely groomed. Life in the cattery pen cannot have been all that stressful.'

Another possibility was that it was the sight of the cat carrier that had upset her so much. When I walked into the cattery pen, I had the carrier with me. She would have known I intended to put her in it, and she loathed the cat carrier. To her, cat carriers probably meant visits to the vet, and almost all cats hate vets.

It was time to do some more rehab. I had to change her attitude towards the carrier, so that she was no longer so spooked by it. The first thing I did was to leave the carrier on the floor of the living room with some dried food in it. For one or two days, the food remained there. When it finally disappeared, I replaced it with more cat biscuits.

Next, I started putting down a trail of food leading into the cat carrier while she watched me doing it. Soon, she was following the trail up to the edge of the carrier and then finally into it. Lastly, I put the food right at the back of the carrier and then sat on the floor about a metre (3 ft) away, staying still while she went in and ate it. Gradually, I reduced the distance until I was able to report triumphantly in the Tilly diary, 'I sat very close to the carrier and she went in to eat.'

In the next stage, I would gently half close the door while she was inside, quickly opening it again so that she didn't feel trapped. This took many more episodes before she was completely relaxed about my gesture. After that, there was no more trouble with putting her into a carrier. The cat carrier that had so frightened her became a place of pleasure, where she would find yummy food. On most occasions, I could throw food into the cat carrier and shut the door on her. One more problem was solved.

Tilly still wasn't normal, however. Her time in the barn followed by a long wait for a home had taken its toll in other ways. In a Cats Protection pen she had, fortunately, learned how to use a litter tray, but she had missed out on the ordinary experiences of domestic life, 'social referencing' as behaviourists call what cats learn in the period after early kittenhood.

That first winter of her life with us, she was both fearful of and fascinated by our wood-burning stove. Flames and heat were probably new to her. There had been no warmth in that barn. I would see her gazing rapt at the burning logs, moving her head slightly as if watching a tennis match. Once she patted the stove with her paw, withdrawing it sharply as she learned that its metal body was too hot to touch.

Another source of fearful fascination was the television. If she had spent her first four months in an open-sided barn, perhaps she had never seen a TV before. She certainly had not had TV in her Cats Protection pen!

Most cats learn to tune out noises that come from a TV set, and lose interest in the pictures. At first, Tilly was so frightened of the noise she would not go near the set. After a few weeks she dared go closer and began to lose interest. 'She is becoming habituated to the TV,' I wrote in the Tilly diary.

However, like some other cats, she retained a taste for wildlife programmes, particularly those about rodents or birds. In her early weeks with me I saw her go round to the back of the set a couple of times to investigate whether these creatures could be found there in the flesh. She is at ease with African big cats on screen, unlike Jess's Herbie, who runs away if lions appear, or his earlier cat, Mac, who used to growl back at them. Soon she was watching wildlife programmes but no longer bothering to check behind the set.

She still hated being picked up. That might have been the result of being grabbed and handled roughly as a kitten. I could do something about that. I started by half picking her up, just lifting the front half of her body, while she was lying down being petted. 'I have been picking her up about two inches off the sofa and putting her down immediately,' I wrote. 'She is now fine with this.'

The next stage was to pick her up to human chest height and hold her for an instant or two and then put her down. 'I usually put some food on the bed so that when I put her down she eats it,' I wrote. 'She still struggles a little but only half-heartedly.'

The final fine-tuning was to put her down only when she was *not* struggling. This was using the same technique as I had done when I ran away from her. She didn't like being held, so the reward was for her to be put down. When she struggled, I held her tight. Only when she stopped struggling would I put her down. She learned that staying still was rewarded, struggling meant she was held longer. It soon became reasonably easy to pick her up, although she still wasn't too keen on it.

The next sign of progress came from her and had nothing to do with me. Up until now she had been very wary of visitors to our house. 'We had friends for Sunday lunch,' I wrote in the Tilly diary. 'She has made herself scarce all day. Then she turned up again as soon as they had gone.' At this stage, Tilly ran away from the post woman, the dustbin men, the delivery people and all other callers to the house.

'It's this sort of thing that makes me wonder how much human contact she had as a kitten,' I wrote at the time. 'She is so fearful of people. Yet she must have had a lot of handling as a kitten, otherwise I wouldn't be able to tickle her tummy. Perhaps she started life indoors and then was shoved out into the open barn when she grew bigger.'

While the taming of Tilly was going on, Ronnie was being visited by community nurses, first twice then three times each week. Tilly began taking an interest in their visits, at first cautiously watching them from the other side of the room, then slowly coming closer until she was almost inspecting their work. Luckily, all of the nurses were cat lovers.

She showed a similar *rapprochement* towards visitors who stayed with me in the small spare room, now no longer her bedroom. Like all others of her species, she was especially friendly to those who had no particular liking for cats. She did not try to get into their bedroom but she would come down to the living room and look at them.

She preferred some individuals to others, for reasons that were inexplicable to me, taking a decided fancy to Alistair the electrician. As he worked in our house all one day, she sat gazing at him with admiration. I have no idea why she liked him so much. He was fond of cats and made chirruping noises at her, but she had spurned the same advances from other men. Perhaps he smelled attractive in some way!

Almost every evening, even if visitors were there, she would climb on the sofa and lie, legs akimbo, so I could groom her tummy. She responded not just to strokes, or soft brushing, but would also let me comb out any incipient mats. It was an outward expression of her inward trust in me.

Naturally, I talked to Tilly quite a lot and she started using her voice to communicate. If we had been out of the house, she would sometimes greet us with a little miaow. We also had the language of touch between us, and although I couldn't smell it, the language of scent. She spread the scent of her cheeks and chin, the pheromone of family attachment, all over the house by rubbing her face against almost every vertical surface – the legs of the kitchen table, Ronnie's walking stick, the armchairs, the edge of the sofa, the door frames, Ronnie's desk, my computer, the wood basket, the television, the phone …

'She's the rubber baron,' said Ronnie, always ready with the *mot juste*. The scent of her affection was everywhere.

If I lowered my head into a suitable position, she would even rub her cheek against my cheek in the way that a cat greets a familiar and friendly feline companion. Many cats have wound themselves round my legs, rubbing against me. No other cat has honoured me with a direct cheek-to-cheek rub.

This gesture was touching both literally and emotionally. I believed I was her special friend, that I was more special to her than she was to me. I had done a good job rehabilitating her.

I had turned her life round and been rewarded by a very intimate affection. Those who love cats will see that I was being the superior human in my attitude towards her. I was the rescuer. She was the rescued. From being an unwanted little ugly cat without much chance of adoption, she was slowly becoming a loving pet. The benefits that I had given to her were huge.

It took the experience of adversity before I began to see things rather less egocentrically. We animal-loving humans sometimes only see what we can do for animals. We can be blind to what they can do for us.

Chapter 10

Who was training whom?

Two training programmes were now in operation in our household. There was my official rehab programme to train Tilly to be the kind of cat I wanted. And there was her unofficial programme to train me to become the sort of owner *she* wanted. Both programmes were doing nicely. Her covert programme, however, was probably going a bit faster than mine. I wasn't smart enough even to notice it was in operation.

I was still focused on what I could do for her, what I could make of her, and how I could change her. After all, I was the owner who was in charge, wasn't I? I was the superior species, Tilly was the inferior species. Clicker training was the next stage in my programme.

Most people believe that cats can't be trained, so they don't even try to do it, but there have been, and are still, a few cat trainers. In the 1890s, an act known as Professor Welton's Trained Cat Circus did the rounds. Cats rode special little bicycles and turned somersaults. The star performance, which makes for uncomfortable viewing nowadays, was boxing cats. They had tiny gloves tied on their front paws and Professor Welton held them by the scruffs of their necks while they boxed each other in a miniature boxing ring. The clip can be seen on YouTube and it looks as if the cats hated each other. Both look very stressed and unhappy.

Most modern animal trainers realize that rewarding cats is the best way of training them. Punishment is a mistake. 'If you upset a cat just once, it will never forget and is unlikely to forgive,' I was told by the late Ann Head, trainer of Arthur the Cat who appeared in 1990s TV adverts using his paw to eat cat food out of the tin.

I had first seen performing cats in the 1950s when my mother took me to a very small travelling circus that had stopped in a meadow just outside the market town near our farm. The act was, if I remember correctly, Anthony Hippesley Cox and His Performing Cats. Hippesley Cox was a circus enthusiast who had trained cats in order to show that it could be done.

His four cats performed slowly and with dignity. Each one sat on a small circular stool, of the kind that was used for sea-lion acts, and wore a clown's frill round its neck. In turn, they would get off their seats and very slowly stroll into the centre of the ring. One of them rode a large ball. Another performed a seesaw routine. As a child of eight I was not impressed.

'They're boring,' I complained.

'They may not do much,' said my mother, 'but it's almost

impossible to train cats at all, so you will never see anything like this again.'

She was wrong, of course. In Moscow there is a dedicated Cat Theatre, now also shown on YouTube. These cats have been trained with kindness. You can see them being surreptitiously rewarded with cat treats at the end of each trick.

In Florida, I have seen Dominique and his Performing Cats on Mallory Square Dock at sunset – one of the great sights of Key West. He puts on performances on behalf of the local humane animal shelter, who approve of him. One of his cats leaps through a flaming hoop. What is truly impressive is not that they perform in this way, but that they do it in the open in front of a milling crowd of people, some of whom have brought along their dogs.

Most cats are far too upset to do training tricks when they are taken out of their familiar territory. Ann Head told me that the most difficult part of training Arthur to eat his cat food using his paw was to train him to do it in a studio with lighting, cameraman and producer present. Teaching him to use his paw to scoop out the food was a breeze.

I already knew that cats are not too difficult to train. You just have to make it worth their while. Unlike dogs they do not particularly want to please their human, so they need proper food rewards. Praise or a pat doesn't do it for them. I had learned that pretty fast when I first trained William's predecessor, lovely, portly Little Mog.

By the time of Tilly's arrival in my life, I had trained four cats, including Boomer. The greedier the cat, the easier it is to train them and Boomer, obsessed with food, had been a bit of a star. It may have been some half-formed thought about making Tilly more adoptable (even though I had already adopted her) that decided me to clicker train her.

I was also influenced by a feeling that in some way she was already a willing pupil. I had rehabilitated her, hadn't I? Now I would complete the process by teaching her tricks. It was a bit of pride on my part. Of course, I knew that no matter how well I might manage to train her, Tilly would be far too nervous to do these tricks if I put her on a stage and tried to get her to do it in front of an audience of strangers, but I had no such ambition. Training her was just some fun for me and, I hoped, for her.

Clicker training, once you understand it, is the easiest way to train any animal. The clicker is a small device that makes a sort of 'click' noise, quite unlike any other noise in normal life, so animals easily notice the sound. Actually, the clicker isn't even necessary. Boomer hated the noise, so I just substituted the words 'beep, beep', an exclamation that he was not likely to hear in other contexts.

The point about the click noise, or Boomer's 'beep beep', is that it tells the animal to expect a food reward shortly. Animals have to be rewarded in seconds or they don't realize what the reward is for. Stuffing a treat into the mouth of a cat doing tricks is difficult to manage. Instead, you click and the animal associates the click with the food to come. It's rather like the tune played by an ice-cream van, which makes regular customers' mouths water in anticipation of the ice cream.

Tilly didn't much like the click noise to begin with but, unlike Boomer whom I was fostering for just a few months, she could be introduced to it slowly. I had plenty of time. Several times a day I would click and throw her a cat biscuit. At first, she would shrink away from the click noise, but she was greedy enough to go for the biscuit.

After about 100 clicks followed by cat biscuits spread over several days, she got the message – after the click comes the reward. This is the basis of clicker training. The click *always* has to be followed by a reward. Tilly stopped being frightened of the sound and began to enjoy hearing it, knowing that a delicious treat would follow.

We sat in our rather messy living room together under the portraits of two prize cows circa 1820. Both of us were sitting on the red carpet. As soon as she saw me pull out the clicker, she looked interested. You could almost see her little brain thinking, 'Mmmmm. Clicker means a click noise followed by food.' Now I had to teach her to do something I wanted her to do, in return for a click and a treat.

The easiest thing was to teach her to sit. People often teach dogs to sit by pressing their backsides gently to the floor before giving them a biscuit. That wouldn't work with cats. If you put your hand gently on a cat's backside, it arches its back upwards – just the reverse of what you want. The beauty of clicker training is that you never have to touch the animal that is being trained, and with cats that is important.

I had the cat biscuits ready, and waited. She stood up and wandered around, looking under the telephone table just in case a crumb or two had dropped there. I was waiting for her to place her backside on the floor of her own accord. That first occasion I waited for about two minutes before I saw that she was about to sit down, which felt like a very long time. As soon as her backside hit the carpet, I made the click sound and threw the treat.

'The difficulty is to get her back on her feet, so that I can click when she sits down again,' I wrote in the Tilly diary. I had to stay where I was for several more minutes before she got up and started wandering around. As soon as her backside touched the carpet again, I clicked and rewarded her.

I did this waiting and clicking over several days, never taking up more than a maximum five minutes of her time. Sitting on the floor with her, rather than sitting above her on a chair, made me less intimidating. She began to understand that if she sat, the click followed, and the food followed after that.

Early on, I started saying, 'Sit,' just before she sat down. This is what dog trainers call attaching the command to the behaviour. I had to keep sessions short. Cats don't like long lessons. William had taught me that. Anything that went on for more than ten minutes bored him and he would just stroll away.

Tilly was not a bad pupil. Over several lessons, she began to learn the sequence. 'Sit' meant she should sit, then the click would come and the reward would follow. I'm not a good clicker trainer because I find it difficult to click at exactly the right time. My technique would have appalled my dog-training friends. Nevertheless, Tilly and I progressed from 'sit' to 'up'. 'Up' is the movement that used to be called 'begging' in dogs. Nowadays, kind-minded people don't like to think of anybody, human, canine or feline, having to beg. So the act of an animal sitting upright with its front paws off the ground is called something else, such as 'high fives', or in my case 'up'.

I cheated by luring her upwards with a cat biscuit while holding the clicker in the other hand. She received the cat biscuit only after the click noise had sounded, and the click noise sounded only when she was sitting with her paws up. So she learned that to hear the click and receive the food, she had to sit up on her haunches.

She enjoyed her training sessions and after learning 'sit' and 'up' she began to realize that the click noise not only meant food, it also marked the behaviour I wanted. When I taught her to 'shake hands', offering the right-hand paw, she would sometimes offer the left-hand paw in error. So she didn't get the click and I would see her noting the silence and remembering that only the right-hand paw got the click and reward. She would then proffer the right paw, as I required.

Each command I made was spoken in a different tone of voice, to help her recognize the different commands. 'Sit' was uttered in a straightforward ordinary tone; 'shake hands' was singsong in a high voice; 'up' started low and ended high. Words sound like 'blah blah blah' to a cat. Tone of voice helps. Cats don't understand every word we say, although they recognize quite a few. They do, however, understand a lot of what we mean by reading voice tone, body language, direction of eye gaze and perhaps even smell.

We moved on from 'sit' and 'up' and 'shake hands' to 'jump'. 'Jump' had an urgent and short sound. I taught her to leap over a little agility bar or, if this wasn't to hand, to jump over my legs as I sat on the floor with them straight out in front, stacked one upon another. It must have looked odd to an outsider. She definitely enjoyed the jumping.

I could probably have taught her all the moves that dogs do in an agility competition – jumps, seesaws, tunnels and so forth – but I didn't go on to those tricks because Ronnie's multiple health problems were slowly becoming more severe. Although his cancer was in remission, his leg ulcer would not heal, he had episodes of poor breathing and the tremor in his hands made all sorts of household tasks difficult for him. I had to do much more for him so I had less time to devote to cat training.

It only began to dawn on me that *she* was training *me* when she bit me for the first time. About two days after teaching her 'shake hands', we were both sitting on the sofa, me on one side watching TV and she beside me on her cat blanket. I put out my hand to stroke her while she was grooming herself and she gave me a small but definite bite. It did not break the skin or even put pressure on it, yet this gentle nip made me withdraw my hand. Tilly, unlike me, was not afraid to use punishment as a training technique!

This little reminder to me to behave as she wished, not as I wished, worked. I started paying more attention to what she was doing. She did not like her washing being interrupted, so if she was washing, I would let her get on with it. She was training me very effectively.

She also started training me to wake up at a time she thought suitable. Sometimes she would just sit near the bed and mew softly once or twice. At other times, when she was really impatient with me, she would jump on the bed, walk up to where I was lying on my side, and collapse into or near my arms. She would lie in my arms while I petted her for about five minutes, then she would jump down. It was so touching. I thought it was a sign of affection. It took three or four occurrences for me to recognize that this was a method of waking me, another training technique, this time a reward one not a punishment.

If I failed to get up, she would try other methods, some very imaginative. 'She woke me by scratching my head gently,' I noted in the Tilly diary. 'It was quite pleasant!' Once she bit my toes under the duvet. Another wake-up method was to leap on to the windowsill and bat the toggle of the window blind with her paw, so that it made a noise knocking against the glass.

Some cats use forceful wake-up methods, such as jumping on a man's groin, climbing on to the bed head and throwing themselves at their human's chest, or even lifting their human's eyelids with a paw. Little Mog used to wake me by positioning her backside close to my sleeping nose. By adding a tail quiver she had a surprisingly effective wake-up technique.

Tilly finally settled on a wake-up plan that involved jumping on the bedside cabinet and pushing off my glasses, my paperback book and anything else that was moveable. That *always* worked. It is quite useful to have an alarm-clock cat, but sometimes I wished she understood that I like a longer lie-in at the weekends.

My sleeping behaviour remained unaltered, since she did not bother to train me where to lie in the bed. William had done this very competently, training me to sleep with my legs bent. He preferred to sleep at the bottom of the bed, and if my feet were there, he had less room. He would settle down, somehow push them out of the way and then refuse to be moved. Even though he woke me most nights at 4am for an early morning wash, I never had the heart to turf him off the bed.

Tillly slept on my bed very occasionally, so she did not bother to retrain my sleeping posture. As all cats do, she established a very firm preferred routine, organized in a fashion that she, rather than I, decided. She woke me at 6.45am and required her cat food to be put down before I made breakfast for myself and for Ronnie. I would have preferred to put the coffee on first, before feeding her, but in order to get her own way she wound herself round my legs so persistently that trying to fix the coffee was impossible without falling over. If I fed her, she left me alone to prepare our breakfast – a splendid example of negative reinforcement.

She obviously felt that I needed a break from working at my computer about every two hours. She would come into my office and intervene her body between the keyboard and the screen. If I ignored her, she would stand on the keyboard, so that my text would be interrupted by random letters. Usually, I would pick her up and put her down on some bedding that lay next to my work station.

Her other training triumph was to make sure I bought her the cat food she preferred. It is a tribute to the power of feline training that supermarkets are so full of different varieties and brands, some of them very expensive. Cats cannot go shopping and choose their own brand, but they train their humans do this for them. Tilly's technique for this was positive reinforcement. She rewarded me with purrs when I gave her the 'right' food. When I put down food she did not like so much, she would go up to it, sniff and look unhappy.

Feline emotional blackmail works. Surprisingly, she did not favour the most expensive brand. She chose a Waitrose own brand, which was cheaper than the named brands. Perhaps she admired the partnership arrangements of John Lewis, a firm that gives all its workers a share in the profits. It is just too bad that they don't extend this privilege to their feline customers! If she had been awarded shares each time I bought the food for her, she would be a cat with a nice little capital sum in the bank by now.

Our relationship was changing and becoming more equal. She now began to develop the frolics that many of us cat lovers really enjoy! She would flop on her side at the top of the landing when I was coming up the stairs, barring my way until I stooped down and tickled her tummy. Indeed, she started flopping on her back all over the house at points where she knew I had to pass her.

I have always enjoyed the feline flop, my name for the social roll, so I would reward her with my attention, briefly pausing to tickle her chest. Brief petting pleased her more than long-drawn-out affection. I could have stopped these attention-seeking flops by just ignoring her and stepping over her. Ignoring bad behaviour by withdrawing attention is the easiest way to stop it. But these antics made me laugh. She had trained me to pause and pet several times a day.

She would come and sit on my newspaper as I was reading it at the breakfast table. With unerring accuracy, she would follow my gaze and place her bottom down exactly on the story I was reading. Once again, I could have trained this behaviour out by simply getting up and walking away from her. I'm afraid I encouraged it by cuddling her. Who wants a well-behaved cat? Not me.

There was worse. Ronnie enjoyed feeding cats from his plate, so she was particularly likely to steal food from him. I didn't want to nag him about stopping doing it. I reckoned he would take no notice anyway. 'Never give an order that you know will be disobeyed,' is a saying in dog training. Ronnie's sergeant in 42 Commando had once made a similar cynical remark to him when he was doing his officer training all those years ago.

After all, I wanted him to enjoy Tilly's company in whatever way he could. So when I came home to see her sitting quietly by his plate, waiting for the next titbit, it didn't surprise me. Her eyes would track his fork from plate to mouth in deep concentration.

'She's stolen my last bit of Christmas pudding,' he complained one afternoon in late December. 'She took it off my fork with her paw.'

Occasionally, if he was eating off a tray on wheels in front of the TV, I would see her strolling towards it with that look of innocence so often seen on the face of cats that have theft in mind. Reaching his tray, she would stand up on her hindlegs and try to hook down food off his plate, using her paw. Sometimes, if we didn't notice, she succeeded.

'Beware the questing paw,' Ronnie would say, enjoying the whole procedure, while gently swiping the paw away.

Nothing is truer than the old saying 'dogs look up to us, cats look down on us'. My own version goes 'dogs have masters, cats have staff'. An extreme example of cats dominating humans was Tinkerbell, a Burmese, who incorporated an amazing food ritual into her daily life. Tinkerbell would start eating her food only if her male owner lay flat on the floor, put his head over the bowl and said, 'Yum, yum.' Another cat, Skink, used to insist on licking toothpaste off his male owner's teeth. Skink's family sent me a photo to prove this. Ridiculous? Unhygienic? Undoubtedly. But funny too. We cat owners boast about how badly our cats treat us. We enjoy seeing our cats rule the household. So it was a joy to me, as well as amusing for Ronnie, to see Tilly asserting herself by trying to steal food off his plate.

Perhaps cats have taught me a little humility. 'I think it takes a special individual to love cats,' says my friend Michelle. 'People with big egos won't like them because they want an animal to obey them. Cat lovers are confident and do not mind obeying a cat, admitting that, yes, they *are* superior to us.'

I was happy to be trained by Tilly. She was making me into the perfect pet human and I doted on this commonplace little cat. I relaxed and enjoyed her 'bad' behaviour. 'I don't want a dog in cat's clothing,' I wrote in the Tilly diary. 'I want her to be independent, like a cat should be.'

It seemed the right time for me to stop trying to shape her life. It was time for me to let her go and be her own cat.

Chapter 11
Letting Tilly go

Freeing Tilly to become her own cat meant letting her out of the house. The big day came when I decided she should explore outside. While she was eating her breakfast, I opened the kitchen door that leads into the garden. Very cautiously she looked out, hovered halfway out of the door, then took her first steps into the big wide world. By now, she had been confined, either in a cat pen or in my house, for almost two years. This was her first taste of real freedom.

She stood about 9 metres (10 yds) outside for a few seconds, then rushed back into the kitchen. Once again, she went out and this time she hid under a nearby shrub for five minutes before running back to the safety of the house. I shut the door. I reckoned we both needed time to recover from this new experience.

I had kept her indoors for so long because I feared that, if I let her out too soon, she would just make a run for it. It is possible to let a cat out too early. Even a normal pet cat, which Tilly was not, may run off out of an unfamiliar house and get lost in new territory. Two weeks to a month is the minimum safety period before letting a cat out in new surroundings. I had given Tilly several months. When she rushed back into the house, I knew that her instinct was to come back inside, rather than escape.

Letting her out, rather than keeping her indoors all the time, would give her a full life. Indoor cats are deprived of one very important thing. For full happiness, a cat has to hunt, or at least have some good substitute for hunting.

A hunting cat is an awesome sight. William was a particularly skilled hunter. Every morning he would patrol round his territory, pausing to leave a spray mark at important sites. By spraying he was leaving a message for intruder felines. It would tell them he had passed by. If one sprayed on top of it, on the next day's patrol, he would learn that an unfamiliar cat had passed that way.

After his patrol, William would move into hunter mode, moving round his territory for the second time, looking for prey. If he heard or saw any small rodent, he would stop and sit eyeing the area. If necessary, he would sit patiently for hours. Sometimes he would wait in ambush for days.

Most noticeable was his autumn weasel hunt. This involved sitting and waiting for several days near the next-door house. He caught one weasel a year, only in the autumn and always in the same place. There must have been a weasel den in that spot, always with a resident adult. He never caught any babies, thank goodness. Perhaps a new weasel moved in when the previous resident lost its life to William.

The weasel ambush was the highlight of William's autumn hunting and he enjoyed every second of the long wait for his prey to emerge. First he sat, waited and watched. Then, when he saw the weasel, he would stiffen, his tail would begin to lash and he would leap forward. If he had to leap into long grass he would jump high in the air for the pounce. Next he would grab his prey in his mouth or use both paws to hold it down while administering the killing bite.

The weasel, which is a long-bodied, slinky animal, would be brought home, hanging from his mouth. As weasels are skilled killers themselves, and have very sharp teeth, William was always careful to kill his weasel stone dead with a lethal bite to the nape of its neck. He would be holding the dangling corpse by the nape as he trotted home. Had he misjudged the bite, or failed to kill it immediately, the weasel could have twisted backwards and William could have been severely wounded. William never ate the weasel. He just left the dead body outside the kitchen door for me to admire.

His hunting sequence of behaviour – eye, stalk, pounce, grab and kill – is hard-wired into every cat's brain. To have a full life, Tilly needed the chance to hunt, to express what scientist call her 'species specific behaviour'. Cats literally live to hunt and, of course, if they are feral, they hunt to live. About 40 years ago, scientists experimented by drugging cats to see if the instinct to hunt could be eliminated. It didn't work. Drugs stopped the cats pouncing on mice only when the dose was so high that the cats were almost catatonic.

Hunting is wired into the side of the hypothalamus, a small area just above the brain stem. This makes a cat stalk, pounce and bite its prey. Hunting is such an ingrained instinct that a hungry cat will leave a bowl full of food to kill a passing rodent. Having killed the rodent, they will then bring it back to the food bowl and start eating their cat food again. The instinct to hunt trumps the instinct to eat. Indoor cats sometimes get so frustrated by the lack of hunting opportunities that they will start hunting their owners. Being ambushed and leaped on by a kitten amuses most cat owners, but it ceases to be a joke when the cat is full grown. The victims of feline violence squeal with pain as a complete set of front claws digs into their legs. This squeal amuses the cat and encourages it to continue the game. (I can only recommend calling in a proper cat behaviour counsellor if anybody reading this is being hunted by their cat!)

I was a bit nervous about letting Tilly venture into the outside world. She hadn't been able to hunt while she was in the Cats Protection pen, and I didn't know enough about her early years to be sure whether she'd had any hunting practice in her original home. I guessed that she had been brought up as a kitten indoors for the first few weeks, and later cast out into the open-sided barn on the smallholding. She might have had a chance to hunt mice in that cold barn.

My garden is ideal hunting territory for a cat. I live surrounded by arable fields that are planted each year with corn or beans and regularly sprayed with weed-killer. Even if the fields lie fallow under set-aside regulations, grass and weeds don't grow there. Set-aside land has to be routinely sprayed with weed-killer in order to earn the subsidy – a mad scheme that does nothing for wildlife and reduces corn production in a world short of foodstuffs.

When we first moved into the house, I noted four arable fields and only one grass field nearby, and I decided to make my garden into a wildlife sanctuary. I planted a boundary wildlife hedge, full of native wild rose, field maple, hazel, hawthorn, spindle and honeysuckle. Berry-growing native shrubs, such as wayfarer tree, guelder rose and dogwood, are planted next to it. The shrubs are edged by grass that is allowed to grow long, in which daffodils, sweet rocket, celandine, red clover, vetches and stitchwort thrive until cut down like a hay meadow.

Even the 'lawn', short grass leading up the garden to a vegetable patch, is full of wild flowers – daisies, buttercups, creeping white clover and other flowering weeds. Conventional gardeners shudder at my lawn, but I love the way it breaks into flower between mowings. The weed-rich area hums with bees, flies and curious little wasps collecting nectar. Ironically, quite a lot of effort is required to keep out unattractive weeds, such as nettles. The garden has been featured in a book, *Dream Gardens: 100 Inspirational Gardens*.

When I let out Tilly, the garden did not look its best, although it was still ideal for wildlife. My gardening energy had been diminished by caring for a 'chronically ill' (our doctor's phrase) husband. The overgrown shrubs were a visible sign of my increasing emotional and physical exhaustion. My tiredness was almost as chronic as Ronnie's ill health, although I did not recognize how exhausted I was. I knew more about Ronnie's health than my own.

Messy the garden might be but there were plenty of hiding places in the overgrown shrubs for a nervous cat such as Tilly. And as a hunting range the garden was perfect. Little round-eared wood mice inhabited the stone wall round the vegetable patch. Small insect-hunting shrews and short-tailed voles lived in the long grass. Less welcome were the rats coming in from the cornfield each autumn. The garden's largest inhabitants were rabbits.

My fear that Tilly might just make a run for it and refuse to return to the house were unfounded. The months she had spent inside the house had made my home into her home, her safe core territory. Tilly had never been a stray and thus outdoor life did not seem particularly safe to her. She remained cautious in the garden for the first few weeks. She would leave the house to secrete herself under a shrub, occasionally moving from this hiding place to another shrub that offered equal cover. I don't know what she was doing under her bushes, but I suspect she was just crouched, tense, watching and alert for danger in much the same way she had crouched under the spare-room bed. Much of the time she would remain out of sight. When I did notice her slinking across the lawn to a new hiding place, she would be holding herself close to the ground in an anxious posture, her ears back and her tail low. This was a cat trying to remain invisible, much as she had done earlier in the house.

The back door into the kitchen had a cat flap but at first she would not use it. She had used a cat flap in the Cats Protection pen, but she refused to use this one. As winter came on, I could not leave the door open for her, so I put a wooden clothes peg on the flap and left it pegged wide open.

'Why do I have to eat my breakfast in a gale?' complained Ronnie. He had cause to complain. The prevailing wind sweeps over the cornfield and down the garden. During this period it carried on through the wide open cat flap directly on to his kitchen chair. It *was* very cold on windy days.

'We have to keep it open until she has learned how to use it,' I explained.

'Bloody little cat,' he muttered. This was just a ritual complaint. Ronnie complained about Tilly, but actually he was beginning to love her. He was continuing to feed her from his plate occasionally, and when I was not in the same room, I would hear him talking to her. Only cat lovers talk directly to cats.

Now that the cat flap was fixed permanently open with the peg, Tilly started going out four, then five, then six or more times a day. Her frequent visits to the garden were short and still consisted of running from shrub to shrub. Rather than staying out longer each visit, she simply visited the garden more frequently.

'She is whizzing in and out of the open cat flap ten to twenty times a day,' I reported in the Tilly diary. 'All this coming and going means she must still be scared of the outside. She never stays out very long.'

Nevertheless, the effect of these short visits was dramatic. After William's death, the garden had been cat free. True, Boomer had escaped for a three-hour frolic there, and next-door's cat, glamorous blonde Siamese, Miss Ruby Fou, had been an occasional weekend visitor, although she mainly kept to her own garden and the nearby barn. Her owners spent most weekdays in London.

Without a resident cat, my garden had become an important social centre for rabbits. They had burrowed under the small stone wall into my modest vegetable garden, emerging at various points among the broad beans and courgettes. I'd covered these holes with heavy stones but some merely jumped on to the low wall and down into the garden anyway. The only way of keeping the rabbits away from their favourite vegetables was to grow them under cloches or cover the veg patch with wire netting, which I did.

One rabbit hole was positioned under the shrubs near the house. Baby rabbits lived under the bushes and would play so close to the kitchen that I could take photographs through the glass of the door. The occasional hare would visit, either to crop the short sweet grass of the lawn or to rest, dozing at the edge of the shrubbery. It had been a wonderful spring and summer for wildlife photographs.

The very first day I let Tilly out, the rabbits disappeared from view. Her hiding places under the bushes and hedge must have carried her scent. Rabbits, like cats, rub their chins on plants to leave a scent mark. The scent of a predator around their territory would not have gone unnoticed. The rabbits were still there and still probably came out, but at night, when she was back in the house. I no longer saw them grazing on the lawn in the early mornings or frolicking in the late evenings. A cat in the garden had made them far more cautious and, as it turned out, their fears were well founded. They knew there was a predator about. She knew there was prey about.

At first, Tilly did not even try to hunt. William had always started his day with a patrol round his territory. She was too cautious to do this and explored mainly under the shrubs where she could remain hidden. She also spent a lot of time near our two parked cars, hiding under these and under the gas tank. Urban cats use parked cars as safe places from which to look out into a wider world. It took several weeks before she began to explore the garden next door and the barn next to it. She still did not feel at home out of doors.

As the weather grew colder, I moved the peg further down the cat flap so she had to push her way out. It meant swapping it from one side to another to make sure she could also get in again. She did learn to use it, although she clearly found it quite an effort. Like William, she would test it first with her paw to make sure that I hadn't locked it. Then she would push with her head. She was a small cat, so it was hard work for her to push the flap, and she preferred me to open the door for her. She would sit beside it, inside or out, waiting for me to do my hotel commissionaire act, but she would come and go using the cat flap when I wasn't in the kitchen.

She had the freedom of the cat flap during the day but at night, conscious of the danger of dazzling headlights on the road nearby and of the risk of foxes, I always locked her in. I had seen foxes in the fields nearby and once spotted one in the garden. Foxes will attack small, ill, wounded or old cats. Tilly was small enough to be fox prey. I worried that she would stray too far into the fields. I had lost a cat once. He had simply disappeared one day at dusk, during a full moon. George, the most beautiful and playful of black cats, had never come home. I never knew his fate, whether he had been eaten by a fox or killed on the roads.

I walked miles and miles along every hedgerow, searching for him, calling him, for four or five weeks following his disappearance. He was missing, believed lost in action. I never even found his body. I had to assume he was dead. I was heartbroken by his loss, and, as a memorial, continued his blog on the web after he'd gone. For me, he lived on in virtual reality.

The risk of a road accident or death by predator is a real one for cats that are allowed outside, which is why some American feline vets believe that it's better for cats to live completely indoors. But I had seen the life of an indoor cat, when I fostered Boomer. It had not been a bad life, but Boomer had yearned to be free. As a disease carrier, his future had to be indoors but I could see his frustration at being an indoor cat.

I didn't want that frustrated life for Tilly. I felt that the pleasures of going outside outweighed the very real risks. She was still young. After so much confinement in her life, she deserved the best, and that had to be a warm safe home *and* the thrill of hunting outside. My other cats, Ada, Little Mog and William, unlike George, had stayed safe despite a busy hunting life. William's tabby and white colouring made him visible from a distance, so I knew that the farthest he hunted was two fields away.

Tilly, however, didn't even go that far. In the first year she explored no farther than my garden, next-door's garden and about 10 metres (12 yds) of cart track leading towards the road. She was always within earshot. I would see her sitting on the track looking into the hedgerows, the nearest ambush sites, which all my cats have used. Luckily, she was frightened of cars, so if any vehicle came up the track towards our house, she made a dash for home.

Slowly she began to establish *her* territory. I knew things were going well when I looked out of the kitchen window and saw my small slummy cat chasing the aristocratic Miss Fou out of the garden. The vulgar cat in pursuit of the well-bred pedigree! Her confidence was growing and, as Miss Fou is twice her size, I had no need to worry about Miss Fou's wellbeing. If the elegant Siamese had chosen to take a stand, she would have wiped the floor with Tilly.

Our days of living in a rodent-free home came to an end shortly after this episode when I found a very tiny, quick-moving shrew, with a long sensitive nose, in the kitchen. Pet cats hunt and kill shrews but they don't eat them. Shrews don't taste good to cats. You might think that this would save them, but it doesn't. I caught the baby shrew, which seemed unharmed, by inveigling it into a Wellington boot, then taking the boot outside. I left the boot on its side in the hedge for the shrew to find its own way out. 'I feel a surge of maternal pride at her success, though a sinking heart at the thought of all the future corpses to come,' I wrote. 'I saw her near the rabbit holes but I think they will be safe until next year. She is not a very good hunter.'

Her hunting technique was pretty incompetent in the beginning. She seemed to think she was a dog. 'I have just seen her chasing a rabbit,' I wrote. 'Chasing it like a greyhound. Cats are meant to ambush rabbits not just run after them!'

She would locate her prey and just make a dash towards it without stalking it. Then she would continue in hopeless pursuit. It was a useless hunting technique for a sit-and-wait predator.

No cat has enough staying power for a proper chase. Tilly just didn't seem to understand how to sit still, how to stalk and then ambush her prey. As a result, in the first month or so she never caught anything apart from that first very small baby shrew, which presumably had walked into her paws! This was the lull before the storm.

Finally, she learned how to ambush and would eye her prey, stalk it, pounce and grab it. But she still didn't know about the final bite on the nape of the neck – the kill bite. Mice, alas, can be grabbed and brought back while still alive and struggling. To begin with, all the mice she brought home were living. I had to keep a Wellington boot in the kitchen ready to rescue them.

Later in the New Year she had her first experience of snow. She had been rescued by Cats Protection just before the first snowfall of her lifetime and had still been inside the pen for the following winter's snow. This time she stood at the open door and tested the white stuff with her paw.

It was just a light fall, so she ventured outside. She patted the snow to see what would happen. One or two dry leaves had fallen upon the snow and lay twitching in the wind like small animals. She pounced on one of these and to her surprise found that the snow was not solid and her front paws sunk into it.

Rather to my surprise, she then walked happily around, carefully trotting along the ruts in the snow left by the postman's van. Occasionally, she pounced on another leaf, leaving perfect paw prints behind her. Her general attitude was one of surprise mingled with curiosity. She was braver than I thought she would be. The little frightened cat was growing in courage and confidence.

Slowly, her territory expanded. By spring her hunting range included regular visits into the nearest field. She also began to defecate and urinate out of doors – I am not sure where. Cats will only toilet where they feel safe, so this was a sign of territorial confidence. She still used the litter tray on wet and cold days but not every day.

By early summer Tilly had learned how to catch baby rabbits. As I am particularly fond of rabbits, I found this quite distressing. William had killed and eaten baby rabbits on the lawn. With the exception of one that I had once found rotting and smelling in my wardrobe, he had usually dispatched them outside the house.

Tilly brought them into the kitchen alive, somehow carrying them through the cat flap. The Wellington boot was too small for rabbit rescue, so I developed a different technique. I would corner them, drop a towel over them, pick them up in the towel, carry them outside and free them in a hedge. Fortunately, Tilly showed very little interest in birds and none in rats. I did not have to cope with a live rat in the kitchen.

Tilly wanted to spend long summer evenings outside and it was sometimes difficult to lure her back indoors so that I could lock the cat flap. I didn't want her to get lost, like George. So I changed her feeding routine. Normally, I gave her a pouch of cat food in the early evening. In high summer, I fed this later, at about 10pm, so that she would have the benefit of warm evenings but hunger would encourage her to come home.

On cold or wet days I had no problem in persuading her to come inside at night. Her soft fluffy fur, without any strong outside guard hairs, let all the rain through to her skin. William had been able to stay out in the rain. He'd come home wet on the outside but still dry close to his skin. Tilly had no such protection, but what she did have was the best of all worlds. She finally learned to administer the kill bite so the mice she brought in were now dead ones. I would watch with empathic pleasure the slow build of intense concentration as she heard something promising in the hedge, sat waiting, wriggled ready for the pounce, and then in a moment of explosive joy leaped in an arch towards her prey.

That joy was at the expense of many small rodents and baby rabbits. She had become an accomplished killer. Ethically, I had done the right thing for her, but it was the wrong thing for all those little creatures. 'If there is a Last Judgement day for animal owners, their (the little creatures') suffering will have to be weighed against Tilly's fulfilment,' I admitted in the Tilly diary. 'I may well be found guilty of poor animal welfare for letting her become a natural cat.'

I was nevertheless glad that she now had everything – food, shelter, human affection and the joy of hunting. The deprivation of her early life was over forever.

Chapter 12

Cats who came for Christmas

'A strange cat knocked at my window in the snow last night, Celia. Can you help? You are the only person I can think of.'

It was the day before Christmas Eve and snow had fallen in the night all over England. It was the biggest snowfall for about a decade. A wind had swept it up across the field near our house and funnelled it into a deep drift down the cart track. We were snowed in with drifts about a metre (3 ft) deep.

This phone call, although I didn't know it or foresee it, was going to be my chance to discover how Tilly felt about another cat inside her own territory. She had chased Miss Ruby Fou, the next-door weekend cat, on one occasion, but this was different. It would be a cat in *her* house. How would she react? Would she be relaxed? Upset? Absolutely horrified?

The unexpected phone call came from one of Britain's most talented academics studying animals. Peter had been an inspiring lecturer when I was doing my late-in-life science degree. He loved statistics, played a violin and was an expert on animal personalities – a man young enough to be my son, but someone to whom I looked up.

He was researching the idea that animals have different personalities and have feelings similar to human emotions. (Even octopuses, would you believe, have different personality traits!) Of course, any pet owner knows that pets are all individuals but there are scientists out there who still prefer to think of animals as furry automatons. Peter had an array of talents but he was not, as yet, a cat owner.

However, when a small tortoiseshell cat asked for his help that freezing snowy night, he responded. He had woken to see this brown cat on the windowsill at 3am, literally knocking at the glass with her paw, asking to be let in. He had opened the window for the snow-sprinkled frozen animal and given her refuge in his warm bedroom.

Once inside, she climbed on to the bed and licked his face, and his partner's face, clearly anxious to ingratiate herself with them both. The next day he started trying to find where she came from, which turned out to be difficult. Nobody in the local village knew about her. His landlord absolutely refused to let him keep the cat for more than a few hours.

One of Peter's friends said she would adopt the cat but could not take her until after Christmas – a gap of about a week. And, to make things worse, Peter was about to go and visit his parents in Cornwall, a hugely long drive on snowy dangerous roads. As his parents had several dogs, he didn't feel he could take the cat with him. He had tried all the local cat-rescue organizations and all of them were shut for Christmas. Then he tried me.

'Yes, but can you get here?' I asked. 'I'm snowed in with three feet of snow along our track. I can't get the car out so I can't even meet you halfway.'

'Yes, I can. Somehow,' he said. About four hours later, he and his glamorous girlfriend turned up at the end of the drive. I pushed through snowdrifts that were up to my thighs with a cat carrier and passed it into the car so that the cat could be safely placed inside. I wanted to avoid the nightmare scenario of a strange cat leaping out of my arms or out of its cardboard box and disappearing into a snowdrift.

Peter turned the car and started off on the long journey to Cornwall. By coming to me he had more or less doubled his journey time on the icy, crowded Christmas roads.

I stumbled back down the track, carrying the heavy box and trying not to fall over. Luckily, the cat was normal sized. If it had been as big as Boomer, I would probably have fallen flat in a snowdrift from the sheer weight. I'm not sure if I could have managed to carry heavyweight Boomer on the relatively long trek down the uneven cart track with snow that deep. Boomer had been a Christmas cat, too, but there had not been so much snow that year.

Christmas Eve seems to be a dangerous time for cats. I remembered an earlier Christmas when Ronnie and I were out in a hired car. Our own car had broken down and was being repaired. The weather was cold and a hoar frost had settled over the countryside, making the fields and hedges white like iced crystal.

We stopped the car in a lay-by to change over driving, so that I could get used to the unfamiliar vehicle. It was a pull-in just off a main road to the West Country, several miles away from any village or town. Just opposite was a farmhouse and yard but no other house was within sight. Normally, we would never have stopped there. I got out of the passenger seat and walked round near the hedge to get into the driver's seat. As I did so, I heard the unmistakeable sound of a kitten crying in the undergrowth.

'I'm sure I can hear a kitten,' I said to Ronnie. 'Wait for a moment while I investigate.'

I peered into the hedge and couldn't see anything, so I put my hand low down into the frozen branches to see if I could feel anything. A small furry creature climbed on to my hand. It was a freezing black-and-white kitten, stiff with cold and fear. It clung to me, relieved to be rescued and desperate for the warmth of my hand. I got back into the car, cradling it.

'What shall I do?' I asked Ronnie. 'It's Christmas and we're going away in four days' time. I can't put it into a cattery because it hasn't been vaccinated. And at this time of year no rescue place will take it in.' My cat, Little Mog, had been booked into a cattery for our forthcoming holiday, but it was a well-run establishment that would never risk disease to the other cats by admitting an unvaccinated kitten.

'Try the farm opposite,' he suggested. 'It may have strayed away from there. It may belong to them.'

Putting the kitten inside my jumper to warm it up, I crossed the road to the farm. When I knocked on the door, a woman with her young daughter opened it.

'I've found a kitten in the hedge opposite. Is it yours?' I asked her.

'It's nothing to do with us,' she said. 'We don't even have a cat.'

'Can we have it for Christmas?' said the little girl.

So I handed it over there and then. It seemed as if it was meant to be. Adopting it at that particular time was going to be very difficult indeed for us, if not impossible. Maybe this wasn't the ideal way to find a home, but for a kitten that had only a few hours to live before succumbing to hypothermia, it was better than death by cold. This kitten must have been thrown away. It could not have found its way into the lay-by on its own. Somebody had put it there – perhaps the kind of person who reckons to make money out of having a litter of kittens at Christmas time. I wondered if this one had remained unsold and was therefore chucked away like a piece of trash. By a wonderful coincidence I had been there to rescue it just in time.

This Christmas, Tilly's first, I prepared feline guest quarters for Peter's visiting cat in the same small spare bedroom originally assigned to her. It has a very worn carpet, so that cat hair, dropped cat litter, or even spilled cat food doesn't really matter. I positioned a litter tray on one side of the small room and food on the other. It wasn't a perfect place for a cat but it was definitely better than being out in the snow.

Just occasionally this small room houses cats who need an emergency drop-in place for a few days. I don't fill the house with cats. 'How many cats do you have?' is a question many people ask me, expecting the answer five or six, or even seven or eight, or even more.

'One,' I answer, and I can see they are disappointed. They want me to be a mad cat woman who has about 20 in the house. Mad about cats I may be, but I am well informed, too. If you love cats, you do not put them into the hellish situation of having to live with 20 other cats. It is acutely stressful for them.

Cats vary wildly in how far they can bear the presence of other cats, which is why I needed to find out Tilly's reactions to this sudden Christmas guest. Some cats are total loners and will not live with another feline in the same house. Others seem to manage to live with two or three others by time-sharing resources and living separate lives in a state of mutual toleration. A few cats truly love the company of others.

More usually, when a new cat is introduced into the household, there is enormous tension. Typical was the situation when William joined my household as a kitten. I already had Little

Mog, who was not pleased at all to have a kitten foisted on her. Deeply upset by the intruder, she spent the first week upstairs on my bed, ignoring him altogether.

Eventually, she came down, biffed him with her paw when he tried to play with her, and ignored him for the rest of her life. In her eyes, William did not exist. William was a cat with a gentle nature and simply accepted her disdainful attitude. She continued to take first place in my affections, slept inside my bed and shared the sofa with me. He refused to compete with her. From this, I concluded that William was quite a remote cat who did not wish for too much human affection; friendly but not intimate with me, I thought.

I was wrong. In the last two years of his life, when Little Mog had passed away and her successor black George had disappeared altogether, William became the only cat in the household. Then I discovered his truly loving nature. To my amazement, the first change occurred a week after he became the only pet. He jumped up and slept on my bed all night.

A week later, he took the place nearest to me on the sofa in the evening, the place that had belonged first to Little Mog and then to George. Finally, he shared Ronnie's bed when Ronnie had an afternoon nap. William, I now realized, had always wanted to be First Cat. Now he was Only Cat he automatically became First Cat. He had been too gentle in nature to insist on this status. He had deferred in order to avoid conflict – as many cats do.

Now in the last two years of his life he had gained the place in my life he had always wanted – close to me. He blossomed, accompanying me on all walks round the property, and spending a lot of time in the office with me. For the rest of his life, I let him be the only cat. Tempted though I was, I did not get another. His behaviour had been an eye-opener for me about cat nature. While cats may *seem* happy enough to share their home with other felines, many would prefer to lead the life of an Only Pet.

How would Tilly feel if I acquired another cat, I wondered. Would she be able to live with another feline in the same house or would I be putting her under unjustifiable stress? She had come so far with me, I needed to be very careful indeed. Would her background as a kitten on a smallholding with lots of other cats make her able to live with others? She hadn't been too keen on Lottie, with whom she had shared the Cats Protection pen. They had never fought but the memory of Tilly shrinking into the depths of her cat basket in the pen made me wonder if their relationship had been very stressful for her.

Although Peter's Christmas cat, whom I temporarily named Jingle, was shut away, Tilly immediately realized there was another cat in the house. She may have smelled her. She approached the closed door of the spare room and sniffed all along it. She retreated a short way and sat there looking at it with interest. Each time I went in or out of the room, she accompanied me up to the door and remained sitting just outside, waiting for me to come out again. She was interested, I concluded, but not in an acute state of hostility or panic.

Jingle stayed a few days, until Peter came back from Cornwall. She was a delightful cat with the same brown tortoiseshell coat as Tilly's, only hers was short while Tilly's was fluffy. Unlike Tilly, she was friendly and relaxed. Instead of hiding under the bed, she sat upon it, welcomed my arrivals into the room, ate the food I brought, purred invitingly and, best of all, used her litter tray reliably. She enjoyed being stroked and, also unlike Tilly, seemed to have no difficulty in dealing with me. She loved humans, which is perhaps why she had knocked on Peter's window in the first place. She knew she needed help and humans would supply it. Peter came to collect her and deliver her to her new home, where I have no doubt she is happy and well. When I'm shocked or upset by cruelty to cats, I remember the kindness of Peter and people like him. They help even up the balance of justice between man and beast.

Jingle wasn't staying long enough for me to introduce her face to face to Tilly, but it was promising that Tilly hadn't shown anything more than a slight apprehension and curiosity about the visitor. After her, was an emergency guest, a black cat called Elfin, who stayed for 24 hours before going into a Cats Protection pen and finding a good home.

Then followed a more interesting feline emergency – a scruffy, emaciated ginger cat who had been picked up on the streets in

August. He was so thin that every single rib could be seen. He was also half blind, and very old, possibly about 16, but still friendly towards the human species despite being treated so badly, thrown out to die alone on the streets when he became ill and unattractive.

Skinny Jim was what the veterinary nurses, who first dealt with him, called him. He was fostered by Carolyn, and then, since she was going away for three weeks, handed over to me for a short stay. He had stomatitis, a mysterious inflammation and ulceration of the gums and mouth. We do not know what causes this severe condition. The poor cat could not bear to be touched near his mouth, and eating was painful for him. He drooled saliva and his breath smelled. He could no longer groom himself and his fur was shabby and unkempt.

Jim, whom I renamed Gentleman Jim to suit his dignified and courageous demeanour, was a remarkable cat – loving, gentle and determined to make the most of life. He showed no signs of his chronic pain, other than not wanting his face or mouth touched. Calm and well mannered, even though he was as thin as a concentration-camp victim, he would greet me with purrs and chirrups. He was touchingly grateful for food and shelter.

He would roll on his side with his paws together, as if praying for my attention. His head would be tilted backwards and he would look up at me, dribbling with pain mixed with affection. When he decided that he wanted to explore outside the spare room and to spend more time with me, he escaped as I opened the door. Then he followed me from room to room, too weak to jump up on my knee but staying within sight (or because he was blind, perhaps within scent) of me.

Tilly's attitude to him was promising. She had spent the first week investigating his smell under the door and looking at him from a distance. Jim, for his part, refused to take any notice of her whatsoever. This, in cat terms, is good manners. It reassured her that he would be safe.

When he was outside his room, as he was a couple of times, he touched noses to her briefly and strolled off. After this quick greeting he continued to ignore her utterly. She responded with what seemed to me to be a mixture of curiosity and good will. They would have been able to live together and it is even possible that they might have grown to like each other.

His stay with me was too short. I liquidized cat food to make it easier for him to eat, and during the first week he ate well. I brushed him and his fur began to look a little less scruffy. Then slowly the disease came back and it became more and more painful for him to eat.

He was due for a follow-up appointment with a local vet, which I was dreading, because I could see he was becoming ill again. Luckily for me but sadly for her, his fosterer, Carolyn, came back from holiday the day before the appointment. I had to tell her, 'I don't think Jim has a future.'

I had to turn my back on him. Jim needed devoted nursing and even then his mouth disease might not go away. I already had Ronnie, whose health was deteriorating, to look after. I could not look after a very ill old cat as well. It fell to poor Carolyn to take him on his last journey to be put to sleep on veterinary advice.

Putting a cat down is always distressing but sometimes it has to be done. Jim's prospects were poor. He faced months in a cat pen with repeated veterinary treatments, stressful for an animal who does not know why this is happening. He was in intermittent if not constant pain. He was emaciated and old. Even if by some miracle he had been restored to health, who was going to adopt a 16-year-old cat? Euthanasia really was the kindest option.

I found it very upsetting, though, because I had wanted to give Jim a chance. His courage and stoicism deserved more, and had I not been caring for Ronnie, I would have liked to try to get him well. I'd have given it my best shot. I might even have adopted him. Tilly would, I think, have been reasonably happy to have him in the house. I knew that euthanasia was the best outcome for him but that knowledge did not stop my feelings of guilt and sadness.

Jim stays in my mind – his purring, his friendliness and his bravery. Cats complain much less than human beings do. They don't show signs of pain and just keep going through it. There's a scientific reason for this. If you are a small animal living in a world where you might get eaten, a predator will see you as easy prey if you show signs of weakness. Even so, this explanation doesn't stop me admiring the fortitude of cats. Seeing Gentleman Jim keep his dignity and courage through starvation, pain and the loss of love was to see an inspirational example. It was going to be an example I would need in the future.

The following Christmas yet another emergency cat arrived. Woodstock was almost as emaciated as Jim had been. He was grey and white, and gaunt, his face narrow with sunken cheeks. His elderly owner had been taken to hospital two days before Christmas Eve. A social worker needed somewhere to put the cat and at holiday time all the catteries were full.

Woodstock arrived in a cat carrier after spending a few hours in the vet's surgery, where he had been checked over. For the 24 hours before that, he had been left in the house without any food. His thin face, sticking-out ribs and jutting hipbones made it look as if he hadn't eaten for much longer.

Once safely indoors, he ate and ate. On arrival in the afternoon, he ate a pouch of cat food. Then in the early evening he ate a second one. Last thing at night I put down a third pouch and he ate that, too. The following day, his consumption slowed somewhat but he still ate four pouches – a great amount for a medium-sized cat. Fortunately, his litter-tray use was flawless – just as well, since what went in had to come out, too! On Christmas day he ate a further four pouches and showed signs of stomach upset.

I began to worry that he was ill. The most likely reason for his drastic weight loss was hyperthyroidism, a disorder of the thyroid gland. If this gland becomes overactive, it pumps too much thyroid hormone into the bloodstream, speeding up the cat's metabolism so that its body is racing along. The cat eats more, loses weight and suffers from diarrhoea. The vet had noticed that Woodstock's glands seemed swollen but the results of a blood test would take time to come back, particularly over the Christmas period.

In the meantime, Woodstock stayed in the spare room and ate enough for two cats. Tilly came to investigate, smelling under the door and sitting outside each time I went in to him. On Christmas day I left the door open, blocking it with my body so that he could not get out but Tilly could look in. She stayed at a safe distance but Woodstock's reaction was less promising. He stared at her and hissed a little before I shut the door.

Two days after Christmas the test results came back showing he was indeed suffering from hyperthyroidism rather than owner neglect. He needed medication for it from the veterinary surgery, and over the next few weeks, with less thyroid hormone in his bloodstream, he ate less and put on weight again.

Tilly got bolder and kept trying to sneak into his room – possibly in the hope of eating his food! Her behaviour suggested that, if I could find the right cat, she would be happy with a companion. Finally, she pushed past me into the spare room when I opened the door, tail up and relaxed. Woodstock stiffened, gave a very low growl, and his body language suggested quite severe aggression. I picked her up hurriedly and put her outside.

Woodstock was never going to be her friend. He was not the right cat to join our household. Moreover, he was not available. In the New Year, at the social worker's say so, he was transferred to a good local cattery to await his owner's discharge from hospital. The plan was that he would go home and be reunited with his loving owner. Alas, poor Woodstock, his health took a sudden turn for the worse and he had to be put down.

Tilly would remain, for the time being at least, my only cat.

Chapter 13

The wisdom of a cat

Tilly was changing and so were we. While Ronnie's health declined and I became more and more exhausted, she flourished and blossomed. It was not just that she behaved differently – she looked different. In the Cats Protection's pen her terrified body language and starey fur had made her appear distinctly unattractive. The glamour of her companion cat Lottie had cast her further into the shade. No adopter had given her a second glance.

Her looks deteriorated even further in the first three months of living in my house. Her fur was matted because she couldn't groom herself under the bed and she was too frightened to groom when she ventured out at night. She was living proof that cats stay good looking only if they put enough time into grooming – a fact that had some resonance for me as I grew more tired.

After being de-matted by the vet, she still looked awful, her fur uneven where the mats had been cut off. Not that her looks worried me at all at that stage. Her ugliness and nervousness were the very reasons I had chosen her in the first place. A better-looking cat would not have needed me.

I began noticing a change after she had spent about six months with me. At first, other people's comments drew my attention to the alteration. My friend Hilary visited us and met her for the first time.

'Why don't you decide she is a pedigree Persian worth hundreds of pounds?' she suggested.

'I think she looks like a Birman, not a Persian,' I objected, 'but her colouring is wrong. If she was a Birman, she would have white paws.'

'Whatever,' said Hilary impatiently. 'If you decide she is a pedigree Birman, then when you look at her she will seem more beautiful.'

'She's not ugly,' said Paul, our next-door neighbour and owner of Miss Ruby Fou, the gloriously beautiful Siamese. 'She's got nice little button eyes.' He started calling her Button Eyes.

When I looked again, her eyes *were* quite pretty, now that the pupils were no longer enlarged with fear. They were not the glamorous golden eyes lined with black that William had possessed; or the slanting golden eyes of black George and Little Mog; or even the large green and black eyes of fat Boomer. Tilly's eyes were small, neat and pale green, the colour of frogs at the bottom of a pond. Fortunately, I like frogs very much.

'Her hair has changed colour,' said Ronnie one day. 'There's more gold in it.' He was looking at her as she sat on the step and the setting sun poured its gold all over her coat. From grey brown she had become a dazzling dark ginger in the sunlight.

Was there a slight colour change, even without the sunlight? Ronnie thought there was. What had definitely changed was the length and texture of her coat. Her soft fluffy hair had become longer and quite lustrous. It made sense to me that a happy, well-nourished cat would grow longer hair than a stressed-out one. Her tail positively flourished nowadays, upright with happiness and curled over, rather like the curly tail of a dog. It was, thanks to her affectionate body language, a very fine tail indeed.

Her tail has some longer, tougher hairs than the rest of her coat, which fall in a kind of irregular spray either side, prompting an elderly cousin of mine to say later on, 'You really ought to plait them, Celia. She would look good with a braided tail.' I was tempted by the idea but I thought small plaits might merely make her look comic.

Sometimes her hair looked quite fashionable. Cats with only soft under fluff and no outer guard hairs often have a coat that separates into strings. 'Scrunch' is the word that my hairdresser Gary uses for this. Tilly, who was now regularly brushed, had a rather nice bib of scrunched hair below her chest. Fluffy hair can never look sleek, but scrunchy hair has its own elegance.

What didn't change was her funny little face. There is a distinct line down her nose, where her right-hand black face meets her left-hand light tortoiseshell face. It's as if her face has been made out of two differently coloured hemispheres fitted together, and you can see the join.

Black shorthaired cats have all-black faces that glint and shimmer in a certain light. Tilly's little half-black face didn't have that sheen. When her eyes were closed in sleep, her face looked rather like that of a small, sad monkey. She could never, except in a golden light, look beautiful. But in my eyes, she was acquiring something not far off beauty.

I, on the other hand, was looking stressed and scruffy. Tilly had joined us in June 2010 and, according to a not very tactful young doctor in the prostate clinic two years earlier, Ronnie could expect to die of prostate cancer five months after her arrival – if he conformed to the average lifespan after diagnosis. His advanced cancer, however, was in good remission. Like the tough marine he had been, he was beating the average.

Instead, a series of different health crises occurred, each lived through and overcome, but he emerged from each one a little weaker. The first crisis was when he fell downstairs and had to spend some time in hospital, when I started fostering Tilly.

What worried me most was whether the doctors were going to operate on his leg. They were afraid he would die under the anaesthetic. I was afraid that if they did nothing, his leg would fail to heal. The outcome was a compromise whereby they put a skin graft on some of the wound and left the rest of it to heal naturally.

Only it didn't. So now a leg ulcer was added to his impressive list of disorders – advanced prostate cancer, chronic obstructive pulmonary disease, a couple of aneurisms, an essential tremor, peripheral vascular disease and long-standing neuropathic back pain. By now, his medication list included eight different drugs, three different puffers and a special patch.

These medical details he treated with cheerful lack of interest, which meant he was likely to forget several of them when asked about his medical history. I was the one who would rattle through the list. Ronnie treated his life-threatening illnesses with the same unconcern that he had shown while dodging bullets during scores of Middle Eastern and North African wars and civil unrest.

He greeted each new diagnosis with, 'Another day, another *douleur.*' Or tried, mainly unsuccessfully, to make the medical staff laugh by saying, 'Fight that flab. Get cancer.' He told the vascular nurse, 'Whenever anybody talks about my aorta, I think of a rather nice little Italian ski resort.'

He bore with dignity the indignities, and there were many, of his increasing frailty. He never complained about the slow deprivations inflicted by ill health.

His second brush with death came when he nearly stopped breathing. By November 2010, the month he should have but didn't die of prostate cancer, he nearly died of a chest infection. At first, I didn't realize what was happening. He didn't gasp for breath, he didn't cough, he merely went to sleep in the middle of eating a mouthful of food, or halfway through a sentence. Antibiotics had no effect, so he was taken off by ambulance to Accident and Emergency and put on a ventilator for three days.

His brain was not affected and I would arrive at the unit to find him hooked up to the ventilator and chatting about military subjects with an ex Royal Marine nurse, who alternated between our local hospital and working in Afghanistan. Ronnie found the nurse a huge boost to his morale, and enjoyed his three-day stay in intensive care.

In his temporary absence, Tilly took over Ronnie's bed (our beds are pushed together). At this time, she usually slept downstairs in the room where the wood-burning stove continued to radiate heat through most of the night. In warmer weather, she went back to the larger spare bedroom. This time, as if she knew I hated having to sleep alone, she moved into our bedroom. Some nights she curled up into a neat furry ball on Ronnie's bed. Other nights, she slept stretched out on her back, as if to take up as much of his place as she could.

I don't think her night-time company in the bedroom was coincidence; nor do I think it was just a question of warmth. Herbie, my nephew's British Blue, will wait till a human vacates a chair and then leap into it so as to benefit from the warmth left by the departing human bottom. There was no such reason for Tilly suddenly to use Ronnie's bed. The downstairs living room with its wood stove was warmer than our bedroom. She moved in with me, and was near me, when I needed her.

When I woke in the early hours, full of anxiety, I could stretch out a hand and stroke her, then go back to sleep to the sound of her purring. She stayed on his bed all night but at about 6.45am, the time when all my cats have decided I should wake up, she would move over from his bed to mine. She would then wake me up by purring loudly in my ear, followed by pushing the items on the bedside cabinet to the floor.

She also spent more time with me on the sofa. I would come back home from the hospital exhausted, slump on the sofa and eat a microwaved ready meal on my lap. Tilly would jump up beside me and stay there all evening.

On one particularly bad evening I came home from the hospital in a state of panic. Ronnie had been transferred from the intensive care ward to the respiratory ward. Doctors there had taken him off all his medication, a big step for a person who was on 16 pills, three puffers and a patch. With the sudden withdrawal of all his drugs, his mind was wandering. I was horrified. I called up the family telling them that they should come over if they wanted a chance to say goodbye to him.

That evening there was a moment of unexpected intimacy between me and the little brown cat. Tilly would never sit on my lap. I could lure her on to it with the help of cat treats but she would stay only to eat them and then move off smartly. If she wanted to move from the arm of the sofa to her usual place on the other side of me, she would jump over my lap.

That evening she took her place beside me on the sofa. Stressed and unhappy, I forgot to respect her space. I picked her up and put her on my lap. Normally, she would have jumped off immediately. This time she stayed there for about two minutes, relaxed and purring, before moving off. It was a little feline blessing.

The same evening she moved on to my bed rather than sleeping on Ronnie's. She wasn't a very good bed companion. She washed and moved around, and didn't have the gift of sleeping absolutely still throughout the night. But her restlessness did not matter, because I was tossing and turning all night with anxiety, trying to plan what I would say to the ward sister the next day.

When I got back to the hospital, the doctor explained why they were treating Ronnie in this way. It made sense. He was also a little improved. This was not the end, as I had feared. That evening I came home calmer than I had the night before, and Tilly moved back on to Ronnie's bed to sleep. It was as if she knew that her close company was no longer required.

When Ronnie came home about six days later, she went back to her usual sleeping places, either in the living room or the spare bedroom. The comfort she had given me was now superfluous. I had Ronnie home again. Could she read my emotions and understand that I was now far less stressed and desperate?

Can animals sympathize or empathize with us? I know that I empathize with my cats and I see no reason why they cannot empathize with me. We can't imagine each other's thoughts, of course, but our feelings of fear, anger or love are surely very similar. Some scientists have argued that animals don't have feelings or intelligence at all. Yet none of my cats have behaved as though that's true. All my cats have had enough intelligence to function very well in their lives, whether it was Fat Ada learning to pull down dustbins, William waiting for days to catch his annual weasel, or Tilly learning how to wake me up by pushing items off the bedside cabinet. All have shown their feelings of anger, affection or fear by way of scratching, purring or running away.

Tilly, it seemed to me, had picked up my anxiety about Ronnie and she had tried, as best she could, to comfort me with her presence. It was during Ronnie's breathing crisis that I began to feel that, although she undoubtedly had needed me, maybe now I needed her. I had been so focused on trying to help her adapt to becoming a good-mannered pet that I had forgotten what she could do for me.

It began to dawn on me that November that Tilly's affection was very important to me. One reason was, of course, the simple one that she was all I had at home. With Ronnie in hospital, I would have come back to a lonely house except for her. Each time I walked in, tired from driving back, she would be there to meet me. She would walk towards me with her tail up, curling over her back, as a feline sign of greeting.

She didn't ask for news. I did not have to tell her what had been happening to Ronnie on the ward that day. Indeed, she did not speak at all. There was no reason for speech between us. Maybe the lack of words is why I felt so close to her. I love Ronnie more than I love my cats, but in some way I feel closer to them than to him. Perhaps this non-verbal bond between animals is something primitive in the human brain, a relationship that predates the human invention of language.

Tilly also helped me during this time by being her ordinary everyday self. There was something soothing about the way she went through her daily life – getting up in the mornings, having a good stretch, going outside to investigate the garden, greeting me in the evening and sleeping near me.

While I was frantic with anxiety about Ronnie, and swept up in the drama of ambulances, hospital wards and so forth, Tilly enjoyed the routine of her life. Living with her was like an anchor to the ordinary, to the safe, to the predictable world.

She expected her morning meal at breakfast time and her evening meal at 6pm and with the help of a timed feeding dish, her expectations were fulfilled. The need to make sure *her* routine was in order, helped *me* maintain a routine. If she needed breakfast, so did I.

Indeed, I could have learned from her. Cats are good at looking after themselves. They are generous with their affection to us humans, but they are also sensibly focused on what they need for a good life. Unlike Tilly, I was becoming less able to care for myself. Although Ronnie survived the crisis of his chronic obstructive pulmonary disease (COPD), a grinding round of hospital visits took its place. If the appointments coincided with both rush hours, each visit could involve up to four hours driving there and back in slow-moving traffic.

Each of his various diseases required a different specialist. Wonderful community nurses visited us three times a week to deal with the leg. There were also visits to a neurologist, a urology consultant, an orthopaedic surgeon, a vascular disease surgeon, a GP and a COPD doctor and nurse. He attended the respiratory clinic, the posh private hospital nearby, the vascular laboratory on the sixth floor of our local hospital, the oncology department in a different hospital, and a rather run-down building that was yet another private hospital. Each expert would conscientiously order different tests. There were blood tests, tests for infection, MRI scans, X-rays, cat scans, oxygen tests, sleep apnoea tests, PSA tests, endless blood-pressure tests, injections, and trips to the general practitioner's surgery to collect his drugs, which arrived at different times of the month.

Another emergency occurred when his face swelled up. He could no longer smile, and his voice was slurred. I thought he might have had a stroke. The doctor's surgery was almost closed and nobody could see him. The best they could offer was a phone call in two hours' time. The local minor injuries hospital told us they couldn't deal with it, either – after we had waited an hour. Finally, we went to the Accident and Emergency clinic. Again.

As it was a Saturday night, the place was full of a mixture of the seriously ill, the mildly ill, the worried well and a fair number of fighting or recumbent drunks. Doctors declared it was not a stroke. They prescribed antibiotics, which I collected from an out-of-hours pharmacist, and about seven hours later we arrived home at midnight. Both of us were exhausted.

Ronnie seemed to be harbouring a series of infections. Repeated prescriptions for antibiotics made no great difference. He developed a couple of tooth abscesses that required visits to the dentist, who finally referred him to a doubly qualified doctor-dentist. Not a week went by without a medical appointment, sometimes two or even three appointments a week, and often at different hospitals.

At each new crisis, I would be flooded with energizing adrenaline. I would phone doctors, make appointments, help him into the car and take him to whatever hospital was involved. Afterwards I would feel exhausted and, just as I was recovering, another small crisis would occur. Of course, being the patient is far worse than being the carer, but the carer suffers, too. Some admirable people handle the mixture of chronic stress and boredom entailed in being a carer with equilibrium for years. I was not one of them.

My digestion went haywire. I could not eat anything without being gripped by indigestion and stomach pains. Sucking bicarbonate of soda tablets one after the other helped only a little. I feared I was getting stomach ulcers from stress. When my doctor finally referred me for an endoscopy, it was a relief to find out that it was just an inflamed oesophagus. A daily pill fixed that. My body was protesting at the strain of it all. My mind was focused increasingly on Ronnie.

In the first three years of caring for him, I'd had my science degree to distract my mind. I'd taken him to hospital and read my text books in the waiting rooms. There had been time to think of my science assignments as I did what had to be done for him. In the fourth year I was still trying to do serious reading, taking heavyweight books on animal behaviour to hospital waiting rooms, but without the discipline of doing course work, it was difficult to retain what I had read.

Slowly, some of the pleasures of my life were withering away as the fourth year progressed. I gave up my hopes of doing a masters degree. Once I had been fit enough to take three-hour walks. Now this diminished to two and then one-and-a-half hours.

I did not have enough time, or felt I could not make enough time, for walking anyway. Two walks a week became one walk a week. It wasn't just the difficulty of finding the time or the energy. It was the difficulty of remembering that I mattered enough to bother.

My focus on myself and on Ronnie had become a single focus on him, not out of altruism but out of inner exhaustion. It was difficult to remember to have my hair done, or even to brush my hair in the mornings. My own self shrank into a small corner of my life.

I became anxious about leaving Ronnie alone in the house, even though he had a device round his neck to call for help if he fell. I worried about how he would manage when I took a whole day away to visit an elderly friend in deepest Devon, who had terminal cancer. This friend had rung to say that he had only a little more time to live and wanted to see his friends before his death. His adult daughter, Louise, who had been caring for him for the past four years, had just been diagnosed with breast cancer.

It was a sad visit and a long, difficult five-hour drive to the West Country. It would have been more sensible to stay overnight but I felt I must get back to Ronnie – not that Ronnie ever made demands. He felt he could cope alone. I was the one who insisted he could not. How could I forgive myself if he had a fall or injured himself while I was away?

When I arrived home after ten hours' driving, I noted in my diary, 'Please God, I hope I don't get breast cancer like Louise did. Tilly was particularly loving this evening. Does she know I need her love?' The idea of getting cancer while simultaneously caring for somebody who was already ill with cancer, was horrifying.

In all this there was time for Tilly, thank goodness – not much but a little. I knew she needed me. My focus was on others' needs, not my own, and her need for my care gave me permission to enjoy time with her. There was always, even at the worst times, a chance to tickle her tummy, put down her food, and accept her affectionate rubbing against me.

'Thinking about Tilly and cats in general soothes me,' I wrote in the diary. Cats do not lose their identity in others. They retain a focus on their own needs. They sleep when they are tired. Sometimes they sleep a lot of the time. They play. They hunt. They look after themselves. They remember to keep their fur in good condition. I would have been well advised to take a lesson from Tilly in the months that followed.

Chapter 14
How Tilly rescued me

I entered the darkest period of my life so far in the late summer of 2011. No life proceeds without pain as well as joy, nor should it. I had survived the earlier desire to kill myself and achieved some kind of serenity in my life. Friends, family, counsellors, self-help groups, a half-believed in God and an accepting church had all helped me to live a contented life. Cats had helped too – Ada, Little Mog, George and William. Now Tilly was to play her part.

That earlier suicidal depression, from which Ada had saved me, had been about the inner pain of an unvalued child. Now the emotional pain of seeing the man I loved suffer was ever present. Ronnie was in trouble. This strong and stoic man would wake sweating or shivering in the middle of the night. Despite a huge intake of three different painkillers, he would often cry out in agony.

He had bravely accepted and lived with a level of pain that would have turned other people into wimpering wrecks. Most of the time he had been able to rise above it. Now a different kind of pain, in addition to the familiar pain, was attacking him. Sometimes he would have to get out of bed several times during the early hours and walk around, just to see if a different posture would reduce the torment.

This final crisis involved the leg ulcer. It had stopped healing but remained static for months. Now it suddenly decided to behave like a skin invasion force. It doubled in size and emitted yellow gunge. Tilly began avoiding Ronnie because he smelled so bad.

In the middle of his crisis, I had my normal mammogram, a check for breast cancer that is given to all women of a certain age every three years. I have always been conscientious in turning up at the mammogram caravan, which is parked in the local supermarket car park. The procedure is a bit uncomfortable but it seemed important.

After this mammogram, I received a letter calling me back for a second check in ten days' time. I was not unduly worried. I'd been called back twice before, as my breasts are dense and a mammogram sometimes doesn't show a clear enough picture. Besides, I was so worried about Ronnie that there was no space to worry about myself.

The night before I was due to go to the breast-imaging clinic, Ronnie nearly collapsed in the middle of the night on his way to the lavatory. I leaped out of bed and tried to keep him upright. He was ill and very tottery on his feet. His walking frame doesn't go easily into the bathroom and I was literally having to prop him up. The next morning, on my way to the clinic, I was angry and worried about him.

When I got there, I knew that this time it was different. They took another mammogram of both breasts, and an ultrasound examination, as they had done before. On the two previous occasions they had simply told me, 'We can't see anything there.' This time I had to stay in the waiting room before being called back. 'We need to do a biopsy,' they told me. That was bad news indeed. Normally, I would have had the biopsy then and there, but the machine wasn't working. I had to wait a further ten days.

Breast biopsies are creepy. With enough local anaesthetic, they are painless but it is weird to feel the needle inside the breast, coring out a little bit of flesh. I had ten of them, with about four or five more mammograms in between. I would have had several more except they hit an artery and the breast started to bleed. Walking out with a purple, bruised breast, I knew that this time it was serious.

'You have five centimetres,' said the pleasant imaging doctor when I asked if she had found something. 'And there are two focal points, perhaps a third.' I forgot to ask, 'Five centimetres of what exactly?' Not that she could have told me without examination of the biopsy results. Googling made it clear that five centimetres was a lot, and more than one focal point was bad news, too.

The size of my cancer was big – big enough to need a great deal of the breast removed. The seriousness of a breast cancer depends on size and whether it has starting invading other parts of the body. Until the results of the biopsies arrived, I could not know what kind of cancer I had. If I had a large invasive cancer, I faced not just surgery but probably radiotherapy and chemotherapy as well. It would be an ordeal of several months and I could not imagine how I would be able to care for Ronnie during this. The prospect of his and hers cancer treatments, not forgetting all his other diseases, was daunting.

Some people take to their beds and weep for a week. I didn't. The early training from my father, who used to jeer at me if I shed tears, stood me in good stead. Although frightening as a father, he had never shown fear. When he had been dying by inches after a stroke, he never complained. I thought of him during these days of waiting. My father had always called me 'the coward of the family'. This time I needed enough courage just to get on with it. I would try to show that his verdict on me was no longer true.

I also thought of Gentleman Jim, the skinny half-blind old foster cat who had remained so loving and had shown none of the excruciating pain he was feeling. If Jim could show bravery in the face of suffering, I could surely try to show the same fortitude in the face of emotional pain.

A kind of acceptance came to me. I was in the care of a power greater than myself, whether that power was a loving God, a natural order, which has no feelings for individuals be they cats or humans, or just the skilled hands of a surgeon. I could do nothing to alter what was happening. I could not control my life and what might happen to me. I could only try to accept it and surrender.

Anger and adrenaline came to my aid as a carer. I welcomed a feeling of frenzied fury. Fear would have stopped me coping; anger energized me. Concurrent with *my* cancer troubles was Ronnie's latest crisis, which required a whole raft of medical appointments. I could not stop to worry about my own problems.

During the next 28 days I had 40 appointments with doctors, nurses, pharmacies or trips to the GP's surgery. One particular prescription for Ronnie – a patch for his neuropathic pain – involved three unsuccessful trips to a local private hospital's pharmacy department where the pharmacist was always out. I never did collect that prescription for him. Of these 40 appointments, only three were for me and my cancer.

By now the sheer effort of trying to get Ronnie to all his doctors' visits, while making sure I followed up my cancer diagnosis, looked as if it might break me. I had a couple of panic attacks, gripping chest pains that I thought might be heart attacks. There didn't seem the time, and anyway I didn't care enough, to check them out with a doctor. I still haven't!

Trying to relax, I took myself for an hour's walk in my favourite Cotswold valley. The footpath runs at the bottom of a hillside down which the wild hares sometimes run right up to me, an experience that brings me a feeling of great peace. There were no hares that day. After only half an hour's walking, I was exhausted to the point of collapse. I had to lie on the grass for 20 minutes just to build up enough energy to walk back to my car.

Somehow I surfed on adrenaline and kept going. Tilly sensed the change in me and responded to it. She began bringing in about four mice a day, most of them dead, thank goodness. Usually, she brought in about one mouse a week. Her mousing success had shot up, perhaps because September was a particularly mild month. The fields round our cottage had been cleared of crops, ploughed and re-sewn. The mice that had lived in the corn had nowhere to go but into my wildlife garden and the nearby hedges. The scientist in me felt that this was the reason for her sudden hunting success. She was bringing her prey into a safe place, my house.

The cat lover in me, however, was convinced that she was doing her best to care for me. Was she trying to cheer me up with mouse therapy? Was it the equivalent of bringing home chocolates for me? Perhaps she was trying to make sure I had proper nutrition – mice – to prepare me for my operation. Why not believe this, if I wanted to? Goodness knows I needed something to make me smile.

She also became particularly loving. She frequently rubbed her face against mine, as if trying to express her affection. Poor Ronnie, suffering from severe physical pain and from distress at my cancer, had turned inward on himself. He was now so ill that he struggled to manage at all. If I talked about my cancer – and I am somebody who wants to talk – he would simply sit with tears rolling down his face.

Taking him with me for my cancer appointments as support was out of the question. It would have been too embarrassing. In waiting rooms, loving husbands supported their wives. If I had brought Ronnie, he would have sat there sobbing. I would have liked to have Tilly with me, but that was out of the question, too. She could not have coped with the strange territory.

Back home, she was my only relief. Moments with her were the times when I felt loving and loved. I knew Ronnie wanted to help but I still felt incredibly upset at his tears. Surely I, not he, was entitled to cry? It was difficult not to be angry with him. I felt he was not there for me.

'I tried to be,' he told me a few months later when he had recovered enough to be his true self again. 'I really tried.' In retrospect, I wish I had been kinder to him but supporting him emotionally was beyond me. He was not there for me. I was not there for him.

Tilly was my prop. Just to look out of the window and see this small brown cat hunting down the hedges would calm me and bring a smile to my face. Her arrival home with yet another unwanted dead mouse was touching, if not entirely pleasurable. Mice were left for me in the kitchen, in the living room and in the hallway. She thoughtfully placed one mouse in her large water bowl, where it floated for my attention.

Except for moments with her, all my life seemed full of fear, exhaustion, responsibility and an angry determination. My only moments of calm were when she lay beside me with her brown-grey legs akimbo for me to tickle her tummy. I recalled how my dying mother had felt intense pleasure when the nursing-home cat had slept on her bed. Now I know why.

One evening I watched Tilly washing herself. Just to watch the ritual was soothing. She lifted up her right leg over her shoulder and groomed the upper side of her thigh. Then she licked her left paw and used it on her face. She then licked her right paw and used it on her face for some time before moving back to her tummy and leaning forward to clean between her back legs.

Next she turned so she was lying on her right side, and lifting her right back leg over her shoulder, she cleaned her lower right thigh and tummy. She then tucked her tail between her back legs so that it was within range for licking. It was the first time I had noticed her carefully grooming her tail. Finally, she rolled backwards and cleaned her chest as near to her neck as she could.

'She is well. She is contented. And I have done this for her,' I thought. A wave of happiness came over me. I couldn't cure Ronnie, despite all those hospital visits. I couldn't cure myself of cancer, either. But I had cured Tilly.

The next day came with three appointments. First I took Ronnie to see a hospital consultant, who admitted him into hospital immediately for about five days to treat his leg ulcer. It was a relief to hand over his care to others. Next I visited the local hospice to implore their help in getting some better pain relief for him. And finally, I went to another hospital to get *my* cancer results.

I was lucky. The diagnosis for me was ductile cancer *in situ*, or pre-invasive cancer. The whole breast would probably have to come off because the cancer was so large, but it had not invaded the rest of the body. With the breast off, I should be safe from recurrence. It was a huge relief to know I would not need radiotherapy or chemo. I made arrangements for my mastectomy.

'Do you need time to reflect?' asked the surgeon when I saw him a few days later. 'No,' I said. 'The sooner the better. I need to get it over and go back to looking after my husband.' Anger, disguised as self-pity, flooded me as I said this. I thought, 'There's nobody to look after me.'

Then, as I drove home, I remembered that there was. A little brown tortoiseshell cat would be waiting for me. Not beautiful. Not graceful. Small because of stunted growth. But with a little loving heart inside the furry body.

Tilly took over Ronnie's bed again while he was in hospital. She also stopped bringing home so many mice, which was a bit of a relief. This gave her more time for me in the evenings. I really needed her company.

I hired a live-in carer for the days when I would be in hospital. If Ronnie was still in hospital, the helper could look after Tilly. I didn't want to have to worry about my little cat. I had enough worries. The mastectomy more and more seemed like just a sideshow to Ronnie's crises. In my agitation I began a mastectomy blog to see if I could make a joke out of my cancer. It wasn't a very good blog but I had to talk to somebody.

I even made sure that I photographed my breast so that I had a 'before' image to remember it by! Tilly sat purring on my desk while I took the photo. It would have been nice to have her in it, her little brown head between my boobs, but I did not think I could make her stay still. She couldn't help me take the photo but she lay on her fleece on my work desk, looked at me and purred.

She was there for me. In the distress and frenzy of those days, her wordlessness was the greatest comfort. Tilly didn't tell me to 'be positive' as, alas, so many other people did – advice that, incidentally, is quite worthless. Being positive does not improve survival from cancer, although the claim that it does still flourishes. I was particularly furious to discover that even some health professionals had bought into this myth and told me, 'Being positive helps.'

'Why should I be positive?' I wanted to say to them. 'I don't feel positive about it. Nobody told my husband to be positive about prostate cancer. Why do I have to be positive about breast cancer?' I began to collect a file of studies showing that a positive attitude made no difference to breast cancer outcomes. This I later presented to the breast surgeon, who, I'm afraid, has found me a difficult patient.

Tilly did not say to me, 'I know somebody who died from breast cancer.' A surprising number of people did. They felt compelled to tell me, in horrible detail, about the death of friends from this cancer. Their reasons for thinking I would enjoy hearing these details are beyond my comprehension.

I didn't need their cancer deathbed stories. I had my own memories from weekly visits to a friend in the last five months of her life, as she was kept alive, mentally confused and unable to move, in an extremely expensive private hospital. Nobody needed to tell me how appalling death from breast cancer and its secondary cancers can be. I have seen it with my own eyes.

Tilly did not give me unwanted advice. She didn't tell me to eat a vegan diet, abstain from dairy foods, or take various infallible anti-cancer alternative remedies. I dealt with this particular advice by simply saying, 'It's too late for me.' Nor did Tilly tell me, as some people did, that by failing to do these things I had given myself cancer in the first place.

Tilly didn't talk at all. She just purred.

The crisis continued. Ronnie came out of hospital with his leg ulcer better but still unhealed. I went into hospital and came out with a flat chest and a neat row of stitches on one side. Indeed, I came out a day earlier than I should have done, because Ronnie was not eating at all. He seemed to be starving himself to death. I thought he was dying.

High on the anaesthetic, I believed only my presence would rescue him. But the first night at home made it clear that my best efforts would serve only to harm me rather than save him.

I slept for just two hours. Ronnie, ill and unable to think clearly, repeatedly got up, unsteady with frailty and pain. I would get up each time and try to stop him falling down. Holding him up made the already painful site of my missing breast even more agonizing.

In between his expeditions, I would lie in bed fighting for breath. When I had been recovering from the anaesthetic in hospital, I had found it difficult to breathe. Now this breathlessness came back. Each time I was on the edge of sleep, my breaths seemed to stop dead. I would force myself awake again for fear I might stop breathing altogether.

At about five in the morning, in complete despair, I wrapped myself in a blanket and sat in the living room trying to calm down. Sitting upright in the armchair made breathing a little easier. It was then that the small miracle happened. It was little, furry and muddy brown in colour.

Tilly had only once before settled on my knee and then for just two minutes after I had placed her there. That early morning she jumped on my knee of her own accord, and curled up to sleep in my lap. For a whole hour she lay in a little warm ball, neither moving nor purring, but sleeping in a way I could not. I did not dare touch her or wake her. I just sat there as frantic despair turned to a calmer kind of acceptance until I was able to go back to the bedroom, ready to help my poor husband again.

From that moment onwards, I realized that I had to start seriously looking after myself. Caring for another and ignoring myself had probably already weakened my immune system. If I didn't take my own care seriously, and put it first at least for the time being, I might end up with another severe illness. My poor husband had advanced cancer. So far, I didn't. The breast cancer was a warning to me.

There would be difficult, maybe even worse, days ahead. If I was to recover, and if I was to look after Ronnie properly, I must look after myself. If I didn't care for myself, I would be unable to care for him. And where better to look for an illustration of sensible self-care than a cat. Since that night, I have tried to follow Tilly's example.

I may have rescued her but she has also rescued me.

A plea for unwanted cats

Tilly and the other cats in this book are all real cats. Their stories really happened. I would never have met Tilly, or many of the other cats, had I not been involved in our small branch of Cats Protection.

Many of the cats that Cats Protection rescue are handed in by their owners, who are devastated that they cannot keep them any more. I have tried to respect these owners' anonymity. Names have been changed to make sure those people who give up their cats to us, or who adopt a cat from us, cannot be identified. I have also changed some other details to respect their privacy.

You can visit all the branches of Cats Protection at the charity's main website (www.cats.org.uk), which will guide you to a branch near you. Adoption centres and branches also have pages on Facebook.

There are so many unwanted cats who need homes. Give a donation if you can spare some money, or volunteer. Adopt a homeless cat if you can. Homeless cats, especially the ugly and old ones, need love as much as the beautiful ones.

And please, if you run a rescue and adoption, think twice before putting down a cat because it is feral. Some cats behave as if they are feral when they are just traumatized by life on the streets and by being put into a totally unfamiliar environment.

Roo was one. Several years ago I was a volunteer for a rescue organization that took in Roo, a dark tabby. He was so terrified he would not come out of his bed. He behaved as if he was completely wild, as if he'd had no contact at all with humans. The charity were thinking of putting him down. Fortunately, they refrained. Two weeks later, he jumped on my lap.

Tilly would have been put down as a feral by some rescue organizations. Cats Protection gave her a second chance, and now she is one of the most-loved cats in Britain!

Choosing a cat from a rescue shelter

First find a good rescue organisation. Beware chaotic rescue charities that keep their cats in large enclosures or just let them roam around, and beware cat-mad individuals with scores of cats in one house – you may end up with a sick cat and a large vet's bill. Some so-called animal sanctuaries in the UK are not even registered charities, so make sure to check out a charity online with the Charities Commission (www.charitycommission.gov.uk) before you visit.

A good charity will try to match a potential owner with a suitable cat, and will usually insist on a home visit before rehoming an animal. While this can seem inconvenient or boring, it is a sign that the charity wants to make sure that both you and your new cat can be happy together. A rescue organisation that just hands out cats without any checks may hand out a problem cat. The best charities neuter and vaccinate their adult cats before adoption.

Don't choose a cat because of its colour. Temperament is much more important. If yours is a busy home, you need a confident cat. Very nervous cats will be aggressive because they are frightened. If you live in a household with young children or with an immune-compromised or disabled partner, you should not take on a cat that is likely to scratch or bite.

Be realistic. If you are out at work all day, do not adopt a cat that needs lots of attention. If you already have a dog, you need a cat that is used to being around dogs. If you don't have much time to groom a cat, make sure you adopt a short-haired cat, not a long-haired one.

Don't judge a cat purely on looks. Think about adopting the frightened little brown cat crouched in her bed like Tilly, the big black bruiser of a tomcat with tattered ears, the scruffy looking stray tabby without a tail, or the sad twelve-year-old pet cat whose world has been turned upside down by the death of his elderly owner. Some charities will subsidise vet bills for those who adopt elderly or disabled cats. However, if you have your heart set on a pedigree cat, you can still adopt a rescue cat from the rescue branches of the respective breed societies.

Don't take the most badly behaved cat in the shelter, unless you are prepared to accept the cat as she is, not as you would like her to be. She may change into what you want, but she may not. Think long and hard before adopting a feral cat and expecting this wild animal to live in your home. It takes a great deal of patience. I was lucky with Tilly, she wasn't properly feral. You might be less lucky.

Don't try to rescue them all. If you do, you may end up with too many cats, and that is a welfare problem. As a rule of thumb, there should be no more than two or three cats in an average-sized house. Believe me, you are doing a cat no favours if you take it from a rescue shelter and it then has to live in conditions of stress in your home, hiding from other cats or living in fear of being ambushed.

If you want to help more cats, volunteer to foster or raise money for your local rescue charity. Volunteers for branches of the larger charities have support and facilities that are not available for tiny new rescue organisations. Don't start your own charity when there are perfectly good charities who could use your help.

Do read up about how cats behave and don't be afraid to take advice. Cats Protection (www.cats.org.uk) and the Feline Advisory Bureau (www.fabcats.org) are good places to start if you want to know more about cat diseases, behaviour or breed problems.

Celia Haddon is a renowned pet journalist and was for many years the *Daily Telegraph*'s pet agony aunt. Her humorous book *One Hundred Ways for a Cat to Train its Human* has sold over a quarter of a million copies worldwide.

For free information about cat behaviour problems, visit Celia's website at www.celiahaddon.com

Tilly, the ugliest cat in the shelter, is on Twitter:
@TillyUgliestCat